A New Way of Thinking

Charles Roth

Unity Books
Unity Village, Missouri
64065

CONTENTS

Activate Your Spiritual Potential

Do you have some problem, a difficulty to meet—a challenging situation at work—an appointment for an important interview? Perhaps you are starting out on a new job and you feel tense and overanxious to make good. Perhaps you have a physical challenge that needs to be met. Or, you may be seeking harmony in a relationship. Whatever your personal challenge, here is a surefire spiritual technique for getting help beyond your human resources. Here is a method for channeling the transcendent wisdom and power of God into your specific problem or challenge. Affirm right now, and at brief but very frequent prayer intervals: *The Spirit of the Lord goes before me, making easy, joyous, and successful my way. I am grateful!*

These are more than mere words. These statements might be thought of as "activators." As you prayerfully repeat these words in the quiet and privacy of your mind, they activate the spiritual resources within you. Frankly, after the first time or two you speak these affirmative words to yourself, you may feel no change. Your inner attitude toward the mountainous problem before you may seem unchanged; but push on. Fortify yourself with the thought that the first shovelful of earth removed in digging a foundation for a building may be scarcely noticeable. But without the first shovelful, there would be no final shovelful. The beginnings of anything that you set out to accomplish may seem hardly noticeable, but actually they are the most important steps of all, because without beginnings there can be no endings, no successful completions.

The Spirit of the Lord goes before me, making easy, joyous, and successful my way. I am grateful! As you persist in using this affirmation, you will notice a difference in your thinking. You will notice a change in your attitude toward the challenging experience that lies before you—the interview, the new job, the physical checkup, the confrontation, or whatever. Perhaps this change in you can best be described by a statement a person once made to me. He said, "Nothing has changed, but I *feel better* about it!" My friend's remark made me smile, because we are so used to thinking of change as having to do with outer things. If nothing has changed in the outer, we sometimes think there has been no change at all.

But the more we understand and experience the

power of thought—the principle that thoughts, attitudes, and beliefs are *causes* and that outer things are but the *effects* or results of what started right within our mind—then we will come to know that a change for the better in our thoughts about the problem *is* a change in the problem. It is a change right where all change must originate, in our thoughts.

THIS IS A MENTAL WORLD!

Some people do not realize this truth. They believe that this is a material world. They believe that things just happen and that all we can do is try to get out of the way of the bad things that happen and get "in" the way of the good things that can happen. Living under this belief, we have built up a long list of superstitions that are supposed to help us to keep bad luck away or attract good luck to us. We may hang onto a rabbit's foot, a lucky charm of some other sort, or we may knock on wood. Sometimes these good luck charms do work. But if and when they work, it is only because *this is a mental world*. The laws of the mental world say that anything you mentally believe, anything that you totally accept, will become real and take form in your physical world. "Be it done for you as you have believed" —Matthew 8:13. These simple words of Jesus are a concise statement of mental law.

We can say this another way: Whatever enters your life is but a manifestation in the outer of some belief in your own mind. For instance, the kind of home you live in, the kind of friends you have, the kind of marriage you have, your job—in fact your total environment—are the results of the kind of mental beliefs you have totally accepted and now hold in your subconscious mind.

Indeed, this is a mental world, and your material world is but the outpicturing in form of the contents of your mind. Knowing this can be a turning point in your life, because it does not take long to discover that *you have control of the contents of your mind*.

You can eliminate or discard whatever beliefs are causing ugly or unhappy circumstances in your life, and you can actually build new beliefs which will cause the kind of circumstances you want to take form. How do you build a desired belief into your mind? You do it the same way you have unwittingly built in the limited beliefs. Here's an example:

Little Petey was told over and over that if he got his feet wet he would catch a cold and be sick. He was told this by his mother, who in his mind represented the highest authority. One day he went out in the rain without his boots and when he returned, his mother was all upset and loudly predicted: "Why didn't you mind me? Now you are going to catch a cold. Better take this warm milk and get right to bed!" And, sure enough, Petey did run a fever that night. Petey's suggestible subconscious mind totally accepted the belief that when he got his feet wet, he would get sick. To this day, even though he is a grown man, when Pete gets his feet wet for any reason, his subconscious mind obediently carries out the terms of that belief and he gets a cold!

Now let's examine some of the principles of building a belief such as this one. First, he was told over and over, "wet feet bring on a cold." This is the principle of repetition. So, one important principle in building a *desired belief* into your mental world is to repeat it over and over. For instance, do you believe that God is your help in every need? You could easily answer, "yes," but do you really *believe* it? Are there obstacles and challenging feelings that could be avoided in your world now by totally accepting the idea of God's ever-present help? One way of getting the belief that God *is* your help in every need into your mental world, into your subconscious mind, is to repeat it over and over in your prayer times and also at other times during the day or night.

Every time you say aloud or to yourself, *God is my help in every need,* it is like placing another brick in place, as if you were building a beautiful new house. You don't have a house after the first brick, nor after the twentieth brick, but you are that much closer to the finished house with each effort. And so it is with building a belief. Things may not seem to change very much in the outer with your first repetition of a new belief that you wish to build in your subconscious mind, but you have put one more brick in place. Just keep at it!

Soon you will build the mental counterpart that will express in your life as a rock-ribbed faith that God *is* your help in every need. Gone will be the fears, the tension over things you are called on to do that may have appeared too much for you before. You will automatically *know* that God is your help in *every* need and you will tackle the things that are yours to do with confidence and ease.

BUILDING A MENTAL PROTOTYPE

When I think of the mental law, "according to the belief you have built into your mind, so will be the outer circumstance," I am reminded of the word *prototype*. This word is used often these days. For instance, I read the other day that an automobile firm was working on a prototype for a body design for new cars. They were building a wooden model that would be exact in every detail. In a situation like this, when the prototype is as complete and perfect as they can make it, they will pattern the actual automobiles after it.

This is exactly what you do when you consciously build a desired belief into your mental world. A belief is the mental prototype of what is going to take form in your material world. The word *prototype* is derived from the Greek. *Proto* is derived from a word that means "first," and *type* is derived from a Greek word that means "model." Webster defines prototype as: "an original or model after which anything is copied; a primary form or pattern."

This is exactly what a belief is—an original or model after which your outer circumstances are copied. It is the primary form (or mental form) of the physical form that is to come. Let's make this analogy a bit more specific and personal. Picture the experimental department of a big automobile concern. See all of the people working on a wooden prototype car. They are measuring and sanding and shaping the wooden model. Seems silly, doesn't it? A car like that would be useless. It wouldn't run. Cars have to be made of metal and have an engine. This looks like a bunch of grown people working on an oversized toy car. But you and I know that is not true. These people are highly skilled and well-paid, and this is more than a toy. From this model, millions of cars will be turned off the assembly line—cars that *will* run.

Picture your mind as having an experimental department. When you go into that department to work, you are fashioning new beliefs, new mental prototypes of outer conditions that will appear in form in your life. Your tools are a little different from those of the skilled people in the automobile experimental department; instead of band saws and rulers and sandpaper, your tools are your faculties of mind, such as, imagination, will, judgment, discrimination, love, and faith.

Here are examples of how you can use the same mental faculties to shape both a limiting, self-defeating belief and an unlimited, successful belief. Suppose you are in sales work and you are not doing so well. The blackboard that lists the salespersons' names and their number of sales is like a terrifying monster to you, because your name is always near the bottom. The more you look at it, the more you are impressed with the belief that you are mediocre. Actually, you are building a prototype of a mediocre salesperson, and streaming off the production line are many lost sales. According to your belief it is being done to you.

So take time to go into the experimental department of your mind and begin building a prototype of a successful salesperson. Build it with words and mental images. Tell your subconscious mind: *I am successful at sales. All the beneficent forces of the universe are working with me and through me, and I am in the right place at the right time to say and do the right thing. Each week sees my*

12

success greater than the last. I am grateful!

Then use the tool of your imagination. See yourself making sale after sale. See yourself confident and quietly skillful in understanding people's needs and selling them that which will make them pleased and satisfied. (Notice that I purposefully left the idea of competition out of your prototype belief. The only person you need ever compete with is your yesterday-self. Competition with others leads to ulcers, ambition, greed, and vanity.) Never mind whose name is at the top of the list; if each week sees your success greater than the last, your sales higher, then your name will surely be high on that list. The important thing is that you are making real progress in your personal unfoldment.

TAKE ACTION!

Once you have started solving your problem at the point where all change must start—in you—the next step is to take action, do what is at hand to do. Prayer is not a substitute for action. It is the silent partner of action.

Here is a funny, but wonderful thing. Even if you should do nothing about the problem except make this affirmation for a few days—*The Spirit of the Lord goes before me, making easy, joyous, and successful my way. I am grateful!*—you will find yourself "feeling like" taking action. This feeling will be a pleasant surprise to you, because one of the symptoms of the worry-syndrome is inertia, that overpowering resistance to getting started in doing what you know you have to do to overcome your problem.

When you start where all successful effort must start, by mentally acknowledging the transcendent and personal presence and power of God, and then formulate this acknowledgment into a concise statement of faith, these power-laden words will activate your spiritual reserves and they, in turn, will energize your will, intensify your desire, and engender all those psychological and emotional changes that make you, as is said, "feel better about the problem."

BE UNDAUNTED!

Let's be honest now, and face something that might occur after your initial enthusiasm and before the problem is completely solved in the outer. You may find your faith becoming clouded over with doubt or discouragement. You may find dark and gloomy feelings arising uninvited from your subconscious mind. The subconscious mind is the repository of all your previous thoughts, feelings, and beliefs. It has to do with the law of polarization, the law of opposites, that when you begin thinking and feeling and acting in a positive, success-oriented way, this seems to cause

14

previously accepted opposite beliefs to surface to the conscious level of mind.

After all, we have spent many years pouring thoughts and words of fear and limitation into our ever-listening and ever-receptive subconscious. But there is one sure way of counteracting the law of polarity, and that is to bring a higher law into play. In other words, keep affirming your faith in God's presence and help, even in the mental darkness of doubt and discouragement. Create balance.

A recurrent prayer statement in New Thought contains the phrase, "I am undaunted in my faith." When I looked up *undaunted* in the dictionary, this is what I found: *"undaunted,* adjective: courageously resolute especially in the face of stress." This has become one of my favorite words in meditations and in formulating personal affirmations.

Prayer has many of the characteristics of a science, and just as a scientist uses vaccines or rectifiers or static eliminators to provide the most perfect conditions for a principle to express through, so in prayer we can use words, such as, *I am undaunted in my faith; I do not hesitate because of fear or discouragement,* to effectively disarm those gloomy, pessimistic moods that appear unsummoned from our subconscious.

Words are just words until we make them ours by repeating them—not repeating them unthinkingly as a parrot would, but repeating them with a purpose, by thinking about them, by giving them our undivided attention. When we do that, words almost seem to change their meaning; that is, they mean so much more to us than the first time we said or heard them.

So it will be with the phrase, *I am undaunted in my faith.* Perhaps it means very little to you now, but work with it. Let those words ring out in your consciousness when fear and discouragement assail you. Affirm: *I am undaunted in my faith!* You can actually feel something happening in you, something good—a confident feeling, a winning feeling.

Success or failure in life can be reduced to two simple attitudes of mind: "I can't" or "I can." When you look at the outer conditions and challenges to be faced and say, "I can't," you *can't* and you won't be able to as long as you stay in that attitude. When you look at the same facts and challenges and say, "I can," then you have taken the first important step toward victory.

This approach to life reveals to us and makes logical to us that we are not alone. We have invisible but nonetheless all-powerful spiritual forces and powers working with us. If we have to tackle a seemingly insurmountable problem alone, we can't be blamed for thinking or feeling that we can't handle it. But we are not alone when we align ourself with universal spiritual law through

16

scientific prayer. We can logically and confidently say, "I can, with God's help."

To sum up, the first thing we do about a problem is to take a deep breath. As we push that breath out, we feel that we are breathing out of our system all tension, all negative thoughts about the problem, all fear, feelings of personal inadequacy, or insecurity. At this point we can say to ourself, "I am one with God, my Source." Then repeat with a purpose the words: *The Spirit of the Lord goes before me, making easy, joyous, and successful my way. I am grateful.*

You have activated your spiritual potential, your spiritual nature. Now go forth to meet and greet your good. You are working with creative Principle, and Principle cannot fail. No matter how dark the way might seem to human sight, keep on, be undaunted in your faith. The invisible force of Spirit is at work to bring forth an answer more wonderful and perfect than you can presently conceive.

Will it work? It certainly will, because you are working with immutable Divine Law. Make no mistake about it, this is a mental world. It is not overcome in the marketplace. It is overcome in your mind!

Conquer
Discouragement

Do you know what it means to be discouraged? Surely we all have times when we sit looking out a window or staring at a wall with a hopeless, hollow feeling in our heart. Our life seems to be so messed up and cluttered with problems that a "what's the use?" attitude fills our mind.

In the word *discouragement,* the prefix "dis" is used to denote separation, such as in the words *disappear, disunity,* or *disease.* Discouragement naturally denotes a separation from or a lack of courage, and if there is one thing that is all-important in successfully meeting any challenging situation, it is courage. The word *courage* stems from a word meaning heart. "Take heart!" the Bible tells us time after time; "Be of good courage." In tackling the psychological enemy discouragement we first want to find its cause. As gardeners know, it does no good to cut just the top off weeds, for they will grow again. We have to pull them out by the roots; similarly, we have to get at the cause of discouragement.

Almost immediately as we search for the cause, we may find ourself naming circumstances or conditions that we think are causing our feelings of depression and discouragement. Perhaps there is a personal illness that has been troubling us for a long time. Perhaps our mate is very difficult to get along with. Perhaps we are fed up with the monotony of a job that we have been doing for many years.

If we should meet someday when you are discouraged and I should ask you, "Why are you discouraged?" you might find this a very simple question to answer. You might even declare that you have tried everything, without any sign of improvement. Your trouble may be with your work and that you have been trying unsuccessfully to get ahead. Perhaps you would feel that you had been playing fair and giving of your very best in every way, apparently all to no purpose. Instead of forging ahead, you may seem to be slipping backward.

Of course, these are major problems, but what makes them worse are the seeming hundreds of little problems that can crowd our life and keep us too upset to do anything about the big problems. Among these little bothers are the bent fender on the car that should be repaired, or the automatic washer that has been fixed twice in the last two months and still isn't working right.

Discouragement may have something to do with the actions or attitudes of certain persons around you. When I raise the question, "Why are you discouraged?" it can seem perfectly natural for you to point to the things, the conditions, or the people around you and say, "There! There is the cause!" And so it might appear.

But here is the shocker: the cause of your discouragement, depression, and sense of lethargy is not in the outer conditions; the cause is *in you*. Let me assure you that the basic cause of your discouragement is not to be found in external conditions, nor in the actions of others. The trouble is not without, but within you.

Now, don't misunderstand. This is not a matter of personal blame or condemnation. We are simply objectively seeking the real *cause* of discouragement, because until we discover the real cause, all efforts toward eliminating this destructive state of mind are just as ineffective as cutting off the top of a weed to be rid of it. Undoubtedly external conditions play a role in the discouragement syndrome; but it is a secondary role, not a primary one. For the basic cause of discouragement, you must look into your own consciousness, your own thoughts and feelings.

One way to prove this to yourself is to recall that two people will react to a similar situation in an entirely different way. A certain situation may cause one person to become extremely downcast and discouraged, while the same situation may inspire another person to reach within himself to achieve a surprising victory—and in the achieving, to grow into a much better person. One person may react by becoming disillusioned; the same situation may prompt the other person to roll up his sleeves and go to work on it. The difference is not in the situation, but in the consciousness of the person meeting the situation. (Shakespeare put it so well: "The fault, dear Brutus, lies not in our stars, but in ourselves.") External circumstances have no power to *make* us react in a certain way. We ourself choose how we are going to react, then we fool ourself into thinking that the situation made us react like that. But when our consciousness is up, the power of the problem is down; and when our consciousness is down, the power of the problem is up.

What, then, is within ourself that may give rise to these feelings of discouragement? The answer is consciousness. In other words, the problem gets its power from you. There are two negative causes or elements of discouragement that we need to discuss in order to change from the consciousness of depression to one of confidence and joy.

The first is the all-too-common tendency to judge according to appearances. We look out over our world and see a certain condition or situation and we say, "This looks bad!" Long ago Jesus said, "Do not judge by appearances, but judge with right judgment"—John 7:24. What does it mean to judge with right judgment? It means to recognize appearances as appearances only. It means to recognize that appearances are constantly changing. It means to see past the appearance, to recognize and acknowledge the presence and power of God.

How does this work out in an actual life experience? Say that the appearance is that you are ill. You have a temperature. Your body feels as if it had gone through a wringer and it hurts all over. On the bedstand next to you is an array of bottles and pills. Over there are the remains of your breakfast tray, which had to be brought to you because your body was too weak to go to the kitchen to eat. These are the appearances. But is that all there is to life? Is life a game of chance where the appearances keep shifting because of some lucky or unlucky factors coming into the picture?

Or is there an invisible life force behind and within all that we see—all appearances—a life force and a transcendent intelligence that is ever seeking to find increasing expression of itself as greater life, better health, and complete wholeness?

A student of the Jesus Christ teachings will hold to the Truth that behind or beyond the appearances of a sick room and a sick body is the ever-active, ever-loving Spirit of God. God is Spirit and Spirit is everywhere present. Spirit is present here and now. God's Spirit is working every moment toward restoration to health and wholeness.

To know this enables one to judge with right judgment. The facts of a sick room and sick body are true; but it is just as true that God's everywhere present, health-giving Spirit is present and active. So when you look past or through the facts and acknowledge or mentally see the healing activity of Spirit, you disconnect your "I AM"—your true Self—from the psychological state of discouragement. You attach your I AM to the dynamic mental state of courage, faith, and thanksgiving. Instead of feeling discouraged, your inner Self will begin to declare, "I AM courageous, I AM strong, I AM unafraid, I AM grateful!"

The second feeling within ourself that will give rise to a state of discouragement is fear. Jesus said, "Let not your hearts be troubled, neither let them be afraid"—John 14:27. Jesus was not simply saying something nice and comforting, but He was explaining an all-important principle to obey when a challenge besets us. He was teaching us that if we want to provide the most perfect mental conditions for God's everywhere-present Spirit to work through us, we must not let fear get a foothold in our consciousness! Remember, the word *courage* was derived from a word that means heart. We must not let our heart be troubled.

What can we do about fear? A quick inventory

of our Truth knowledge will tell us that love is the supreme remedy of fear. "Perfect love casts out fear"—I John 4:18. If, therefore, we fill our hearts and thoughts with love, then fear thoughts which lead to discouragement must of necessity disappear.

Try a little experiment: When you are alone, say these words to a hypothetical other person, "I am afraid of you." Then say to the same hypothetical person, "I love you." Notice the subtle difference in your consciousness. When you say, "I am afraid of you," you can actually feel a disturbing current in you and around you. When I tried the experiment, I felt a kind of disturbing tingling in my hands and a feeling that they were about to perspire. When you say, "I love you," you feel an altogether different current. A kind of peace envelopes you; a relaxing, harmonizing feeling enfolds you.

If you can actually sense or feel a definite disconcerting reaction when you place your attention on the word *fear*, and a definite harmonizing response when you place your attention on the word *love*, then you can plainly see how your state of discouragement, rooted in fear, can directly affect your body in a negative way. Conversely, it is plain that filling your consciousness with calmness and love and faith has a direct positive effect on your physical organism.

When you are discouraged, stop yourself from

recounting the outer troubles that you feel are the cause of your painful, negative outlook. Stop wishing that certain people would get out of your life, or that certain circumstances would change, or that you could get away from it all. You do not need a change of environment as much as you need a change of heart. Take heart! Take courage! Affirm loud and clear so that your subconscious mind gets the message, *There is nothing to fear, for God is here*!

Then affirm good and strong so that the subconscious mind is aroused to work constructively with you: *I refuse to be cowed by or to knuckle under to these conditions that presently exist in my life. I am a child of God. I am a free spiritual being. I have the potential to stand up to these conditions and with God's help to change their effect on me. I am grateful!*

What can you do to implement this realization in your life? The first thing is to be aware and to act on the awareness that you are not alone and helpless. You are more than the flesh and blood form that is reflected back at you from your mirror. Within that form, animating that form, is an invisible you.

What is this *you* made of? It is made of life, Spirit. (The word *spirit* comes from the Latin "spiritus," meaning breath or life.) In other words, you are a spiritual being; a center of life, livingness.

Where do you get your life? What is its source? Here is where God comes into the picture. God is that universal Life, that universal *I AM* which is living through, and as, you and me and every other living thing.

That may seem a bit deep, but if we are going to start our ascent out of the pit of discouragement with the idea that no one is alone and helpless, we have to have a firm basis for saying and believing this Truth. We have to have a Source, a God, that we can really believe in.

For too long people have thought of God as a bearded man on a throne in the heavens. Such a concept of God is fine when things are going along all right; but when we run into real personal trouble, it is difficult to believe that such a God has the time to help us straighten out all our comparatively trivial problems.

But when we understand God to be what Jesus taught Him to be—Spirit—then we have a God who is very close by, not a divine person busy running the world from a throne in the sky, but a spiritual Presence that is the very Life of our life. God is so very close to us and conscious of us and our problems, large and small, that the poet Tennyson was inspired to write, "Closer is He than breathing, and nearer than hands and feet" ("A Higher Pantheism").

Because you are a point of expression of that universal creative Spirit that we call God, the next step is for you to provide the most perfect mental conditions for this universal power to express through.

Did you ever try to water your lawn while you were standing on the hose? That gives you a graphic picture of a person—of yourself—wanting God's power to flow through to help solve a problem, yet blocking the flow with thoughts and feelings that are negatively oriented. This is what happens when you believingly say: "It will never work out." "What's the use?" "I'm a born loser."

How are you going to change those negative thought-blocks? How can we shake ourself loose from those kinds of thoughts and feelings? It sounds easy, but as you and I know from painful experience, it isn't always as easy as it sounds. Still, the outcome is certain if we *hold to the Truth*, for God is always ready to outpour His divine nature into our experience.

God is ready, willing, and able.

Life is ready, willing, and receptive to being acted upon by the formative power of God.

There remains only for us to clear the way mentally.

Here is a technique that has been found extremely helpful and effective in releasing those negative concepts that limit fulfillment. It is simple, but it takes thought and practice to work fully.

Let's start from the bottom of the pit. There you are in the middle of a real problem that has you tense and jittery. You can't eat, you can't sleep. The problem is all you think about and its tentacles of tension seem to reach right out into your physical body, keeping you from being able to do anything but sit and stare at the wall or carpet.

Now take a break from your thought about the problem as it presently looks, and *pretend* for a while. Pretend that somehow, magically, days or months have slipped by and it is now some future time and your problem has worked out in a marvelous way. Get the feeling that you are able to say: "The problem no longer exists, it worked out in a way that I never imagined. It's over now and I feel happy and grateful that everything worked out so wonderfully for all concerned."

Follow that "feeling" of the completed and perfect outworking with the spiritual logic that such a daydream of a perfect answer isn't impossible if you really believe God is near. Would that daydream, or anything, be impossible to such a power as God? Of course it wouldn't!

There is the possibility, then, of your "pretending" coming true! The inner thought and feeling of possibility is the mustard seed of which Jesus spoke.

Now you can return to facing your problem positively. You will find that your attitude is indeed changed toward it. Some of the hopeless-

28

ness and discouragement have disappeared, and you are stronger. For a few days to come, when you think about the problem take a brief instant to pretend again that time has raced by and the problem is behind you—solved in a wonderful way.

Don't try to picture exactly how it all worked out. Leave that to God. Just picture or imagine how you *feel* about its perfect outworking. Then silently breathe the simple prayer, "Thank You, Father."

The really thrilling part of this technique comes with the day that the problem is behind you and has been worked out in an easy, natural, wonderful way. How good you feel, how proud you are of yourself that you had the courage to stand firm in your faith even when the appearances were darkest!

The next time some problem has you discouraged and upset, use the "pretending technique." Pretend the challenge is over and done, that God has worked it out in a perfect way, for He can and He will, if only you will open the way with even a mustard-seed faith.

Get Rid of Guilt

When we approach Christianity as a practical teaching, instead of as a religious organization or institution, we find that we are continually learning more about ourself, about life, and about God. Truth is not something static, something we join and pay our dues to, something that entitles us after dying to go to a place where there are streets of gold, angelic music, and no worries.

The very word *life* implies growth. When we stop growing physically, life does not stop; we are destined to continue growing mentally and spiritually. The teachings of Jesus offer us the framework, the help to grow spiritually, unfolding the Christ of our being that has been enfolded within our soul-nature from the beginning of time.

In order to free this essential growth process, we need to understand and release the limitations that we have placed upon ourself through error-thinking. Surely a perennial error-thought of mankind and a major impediment to our soul unfoldment is the concept of guilt. A letter I once received seemed to capsulize this problem. The writer explained: "How do I keep from 'kicking myself' for worldly mistakes? I have tried saying to myself, 'This just goes to show that I am not God, that I am far from perfect.' So I try a little harder to give the situation my undivided attention and common sense, often just to find myself becoming more tense, therefore making more errors. I can't get rid of this guilty feeling."

As we "feel with" the writer of this letter, surely we can each supply a personal example of such a human error from our own life. Have you ever felt like kicking yourself for a mistake? Then perhaps you have said to yourself words to this effect, "This just goes to show that I'm not perfect." Then have you tried harder to avoid making a similar mistake, and gotten tense and worried, therefore making more human errors or more trouble for yourself?

Let's translate these everyday words into the principles they represent. For instance, the words *kicking yourself* imply a basically good principle—the principle of repentance. What does a person really mean when he says, "I feel like kicking myself"? He means that he very plainly and vividly is aware of his mistake—the wrongness of it, the foolishness of it. He sees this so painfully that he never wants to do a wrong, foolish, illogical, harmful thing like that again.

This is exactly what repentance is: recognizing, acknowledging a wrong action and feeling sorry about it. So kicking yourself figuratively is fine. It indicates humility, an inner honest admission of your human limitations, your human inability to meet the situation successfully and correctly.

So far you are doing just fine! You have repented of your mistake (or sin if you want to call it that; for sin is a missing of the mark that you know you should aim for). And you are humble enough to admit that with God's help, you could take better aim next time.

But what happens next is the crucial part. Do you maintain this attitude of humility, admitting your own human limitation and enlisting the help of the transcendent Presence and wisdom of God? Or do you go right back to running your life yourself and kicking yourself when you get into trouble?

Many people use this mental device of kicking themselves as a kind of self-inflicted punishment. And, of course, once they have been punished (that is, once they have punished *themselves* through the painful experience of feeling like kicking themselves), they feel they have paid the penalty and are free to do whatever they please again.

As a child you may have thrown apples at the high windows of your grandfather's barn and broken several of the panes. If you were caught and you got your "talking to" or your "walloping," then the case was closed. Everything was then even—you were free to do something similar again, for which, if caught, you would pay the penalty and be in the clear once more.

Often we carry this false logic into adult life and that is why many people make such a fuss of suffering over mistakes of commission or omission. Like the little child being lectured or spanked for the apple-throwing, their inner anguish is making up for the mistake. When they feel the punishment is enough to suit the "crime," they stop suffering and feel okay again.

We can see this in the letterwriter's statement, "So I try a little harder, just to find myself becoming more tense, therefore making more errors." Obviously, such an individual hasn't changed yet; he has merely tried to erase the mistake by submitting to self-punishment and self-criticism. The answer to the question of how to get rid of a guilty feeling is to follow the urge to repent and to admit humility—the admission that we aren't so smart and that we need the help of a wisdom greater than our own—with a deep and sincere resolution to follow God's inner guidance from that point on!

There is a difference between feeling right and being right. When you kick yourself and suffer the pains of the "damned," that is, when you pay the penalty according to the personal ego's standards, then you may feel all right, but you won't *be* right.

The only way you are going to be right is to admit the mistake, acknowledge your human helplessness, and make up your mind to look to God's guidance from that point on. Then wait for the next time circumstances similar to those which triggered your previous mistake arise. If you then look to and follow the guidance of the Light within, instead of losing control and doing whatever it was that you did before in error, then and only then can you be sure that your former repentance not only made you feel right, but that it set you right, too!

There is a subtle but deep point to this lesson. We are prone to balance sin with punishment. We feel that punishment erases the mistake. A person steals a loaf of bread; he sits in jail for six months. The teenager keeps the car out longer than his parents' deadline; he is grounded for a week. You get angry at someone only to find out that it wasn't his fault at all, so you make yourself suffer an appropriate amount of time by kicking yourself, an emotionally masochistic device.

But in the science of living, in rising above the human-animal octave of life and reaching for the higher octave of unfolding the seed of divinity within you, the basic principle is *change*, not punishment. The thing that negates or erases a mistake of any kind is not punishment, but change. You have to change or there is no advance, no growth.

How can you change unless life offers you another experience in which you are tempted to make the same mistake? If you yield to the temptation and make the same mistake, you haven't changed and you haven't grown. However, if you are offered another experience in which you are tempted to make the same mistake and you do not yield to the temptation, but follow instead that inner guidance as to the right thing to do, then you have changed for the better. Then and only then is the previous mistake forgiven, erased.

To err is human; to forgive your growing, learning self and to repent is divine.

Guilt is a destructive emotion. It is not a virtue. Guilt is a self-punishing device that we foolishly think will even the score and make us feel good again. But it never does. We go on making the same mistakes, and the guilt multiplies.

We need to depend on God for guidance, not on our own vain, little self. Then if we do make a mistake we will feel sorry, humble, determined to renew our efforts to depend on God—but we won't feel guilty.

We sometimes ask God to forgive us, to take away our guilt. But how can He? He doesn't see us as guilty. He only sees us as having made a mistake in our unfolding patterns and He says, in effect, "That's all right, beloved Child, you made a mistake, but you are innocent in Spirit. Next time let Me help you express your true nature!"

The divine Father is always forgiving, never punishing. But we have to realize His divine nature in order to accept His forgiving, freeing love. Too often we associate negative experience we have had with our earthly fathers to our *infinite* Father, and we get a false notion of divine forgiveness.

When you were a child, did you ever have the experience of doing something wrong—perhaps like secretly taking some object home with you from a house you were visiting, something that didn't belong to you? And then did your parents find out and say with outraged feelings, "Shame on you! That's stealing. You naughty, naughty child, shame on you!"?

Or perhaps your curiosity got you into trouble and again came the parental cry: "You ought to be ashamed of yourself. Just wait until your father comes home. He will teach you something you won't forget." The father's "teaching" was probably a good sound thrashing. This, of course, is not a teaching at all, but a punishment.

Psychologists tell us that even though these childhood experiences are usually long-forgotten by parents, and even seem to be forgotten by the children now grown up, they may still exist in the subconscious level of mind as a poisonous pool of guilt. Guilt is the silent destroyer, but we can get rid of it!

Unfortunately an unenlightened interpretation of Christianity can add to our problem of guilt, rather than lessen it—this in spite of the fact that Jesus' teachings, the heart of Christianity, tell of God's infinite love and infinite capacity for forgiveness.

It has been said that many persons think of God as they have thought of their human father; the one who "teaches us a lesson we won't forget" when we humanly fail to live up to what we feel are his standards. Except God has great advantage over our human father—God can see into our innermost thoughts, so we may feel there is no escape from His retribution.

Remember the story of the little boy who was getting into some childish mischief in the back yard when his mother's voice came from the kitchen window, "Jimmy, just what do you think you're doing?"

"Gosh," little Jimmy muttered, "between Mom and Santa Claus and God, a fellow is always being watched."

Let's think this through. Even though Jesus refers to God as our Father, does it naturally follow that punishment is God's way of teaching? How are you going to teach someone the multiplication tables by punishing him? How do you teach patience or good manners or faith in God—by punishing? Teaching is always a constructive approach. Punishment can be a destructive experience.

If you try to step to the ground right off the roof of your house, instead of using a ladder, the law of gravity will operate in such a way that you will probably be injured. Does the law of gravity *punish* you? Or is your painful and negative experience caused by either your own ignorance of the law of gravity or your carelessness in obeying its requirements? We are not punished for our sins or mistakes, but by them.

This is a universe of spiritual law. When through ignorance, willfulness, or carelessness we fail to comply with the requirements of spiritual law, we bring hurt and pain to ourself.

One of the greatest practical lessons on forgiveness in the New Testament has been overlooked by most Bible readers and teachers. Jesus was celebrating the Passover with His disciples and good friends and He told them of His coming betrayal and execution. Peter—boasting Peter, the big fisherman—loudly proclaimed that *he* would never desert the Master, that he would be glad to die for Him if necessary. However, within twenty-four hours Peter had flatly denied that he even knew Jesus—denied not once, but three times!

How great must have been Peter's shame, his guilt. Jesus' friends felt devastated at His seeming death on the cross; but Peter must have felt a special guilt, a unique wretchedness. This type of guilt has been duplicated in the lives of many persons. A dear one passes on and we remember that shortly before the passing we were mean or neglectful to that loved one. What a painful suffering that is. Every thought of love that springs to our heart for our loved one is clouded by an accusing voice within us that says, "If you had really loved, how could you have done the things you did?" And so we spend our time and energy in suffering and in wishing we could turn back the clock and undo our past mistakes. But now let us see how this awful feeling of guilt was washed from Peter's consciousness.

The joyful day came when the disciples discovered that Jesus had indeed conquered the last enemy, death. How happy they all must have been! But perhaps Peter's happiness was reserved. We can picture him with a forced smile on his face; underneath he may have been reliving over and over again those three tortuous memories of his denial of Jesus. Jesus was probably well aware of Peter's averted eyes and of the suffering going on in Peter's heart. And so one day He took Peter for a walk and while they were strolling along that beautiful countryside around the Sea of Galilee, Jesus said to Peter, "Peter, do you love me?" Peter answered, "Yes, Lord; you know that I love you." And Jesus replied, "Feed my lambs"—John 21:15. The Bible reader is usually perplexed at what happens next. Jesus asks Peter the same question two more times. And Peter answers the same way each time, but with growing feeling. Jesus always gives the same kind of reply: "Tend my sheep . . . Feed my sheep"—John 21:16, 17.

Do you begin to see the connection? Peter denied Jesus three times and no doubt felt tremendously guilty about it. Here Jesus is giving him the opportunity to *affirm his love three times* with growing conviction and feeling. The mistake or sin was nullified or washed out of Peter's consciousness by a reaffirmation of his love for Jesus!

This is the secret of self-forgiveness, the secret of washing out of our consciousness those poisonous pools of guilt about mistakes that can't be changed because time simply cannot turn backward. It is this: start today, right now, right where you are, to do what you know to be the right thing.

"Feed my sheep," Jesus told Peter. This obviously means not to look backward. Forget your past mistakes. Remembering them only diminishes your ability to live productively in the present. Instead, put your whole attention on the task at hand and on doing it with the very best that is in you.

Peter probably thought he deserved punishment, and there is a sense in which he might have thought he would feel better if he were punished—sort of paying for his guilt. Many of us today look for ways to punish ourself, feeling that we deserve punishment for some of our awful mistakes; and some persons get a warped satisfaction out of their suffering. But this is not Jesus' way!

Jesus knew that the only time there is, is *now*. The past is done, the future is not yet born. And what the future will be is determined by our actions, feelings, and thoughts in the now. So if you are harboring a feeling of guilt, reaffirm the truth about yourself. Say to yourself: *The truth is that I am a child of God—now! I love God and I love my fellowman—now! I can undo my past mistakes by living and acting now to my highest conception of how a child of God will act.*

Remember that wonderful passage in the Old Testament, "I will restore to you the years which the swarming locust has eaten"—Joel 2:25. When you look out at the barren and stripped fields after a horde of locusts has passed through it, it seems impossible that those fields could be restored to their former greenness.

When you look back at the wasted years before you came into an understanding of Truth, before you learned that every "sin," every mistake can be expiated by an act of love now, by living up to the very best that you know now, you might think, How can those wasted years ever be restored?

41

But they can! You will find yourself living so fully, so fulfillingly in the present that those years will fade away from memory. If you think of them at all, it will be to bless them for having been the means by which you were brought to this present moment of God-centered living.

Not long ago I saw a documentary on television on the subject of guilt. The learned and lettered psychologists gave an excellent description of guilt and its causes in childhood, adolescence, and maturity. But they seemed to conclude that guilt is something we have to live with, something that can be turned into good if it motivates us to do charitable and (on the surface) loving acts. I don't agree. Doing a loving act out of a motive of atoning for our guilt is selfish, not loving, and an act cannot be selfish and loving at the same time, for love means selflessness. We would not be getting rid of our guilt at all that way, we would be satisfying its greedy appetite for a time.

The positive way to get rid of guilt, once and for all, is to forget the past, forgive the past. Start today to live from the direct motivation of Spirit within you and the pools of guilt will evaporate in the warmth of your true love of God, of yourself, and of others. Live and express in the now as you are now in Spirit—a perfect, free, and eternally beloved child of God.

Respond to Stress

The main thrust of practical Christianity is to relate the principles of spirituality that are found in the Bible to everyday problems—including tension, nervousness, and worry.

We can easily find many reasons for tensions: the rising cost of living, the unpredictable stock market averages, the pressure of competition in business, and the news media filled with graphic headlines of the sad state of the world. It is no wonder that many persons gulp tranquilizers and that others use reality-escaping drugs. But the main body of us keeps trying to make it through each day in the best way we can, gathering ulcers sometimes, perhaps even developing high blood pressure and nervous exhaustion on our way, if we have not yet learned to cope constructively with life.

Does practical Christianity have an answer for us? I strongly feel that it does. The answer is like the experience of a little girl who didn't want to go to bed one night when her mother told her to because she said she had "some thinking to do." Her understanding mother told her to finish her thinking and then to go on to bed. Later the mother asked the girl, "What were you thinking about, dear?"

The little girl confided, "I was thinking about gravity, Mother, and I decided that gravity is God right at the center of the world, keeping the people right side up when the world is upside down."

This certainly is a simple statement of a profound Truth! God is that spiritual stabilizer within us that will always keep us upright, peaceful, and poised if we will just let go and let God, if we will trust God in the same unquestioning way that we trust the universal principle of gravity.

The spiritual principle that will enable you to face the constant bombardment of tension-provoking experiences in your life is this: *What happens around you or to you isn't nearly as important as your* response *to what happens to you and around you!* Your mental and emotional reaction is what gives a circumstance the power to hurt you or help you.

There is a way in which you can set up what we might call a "spiritual energy field" within and around you—a kind of force field that will act as a shock absorber to protect you from the pressures, stress, and nerve-shattering demands of your environment. Such a spiritual energy field is desperately needed today, and the need for it will increase a hundredfold as life grows in outer complexity.

The key word to today's pressure-filled environment is *change.* Things change so quickly, so often! Old jobs are done away with because of new discoveries; as a result, people change jobs or change the way they do their jobs.

Even our homes, the places where family roots are put down, are affected. Nationwide companies transfer their workers from city to city. Increasing numbers of people live in apartments and move more often. Homeowning has changed in that people keep buying better-looking or larger homes as their incomes increase.

Our food changes. I once read that seventy-five percent of the items in the supermarkets today were not on the shelves just ten years ago. Ways of preparing food change. We don't always boil potatoes and mash them with a wooden mallet anymore; instead, we can add water to dried flakes and *presto*—mashed potatoes. We can cook foods still in cellophane bags and whole dinners are frozen, ready for us to pop into the oven.

Just think of the many other changes in the last ten years! And these won't stop now—change is like a snowball rolling downhill. The human mind, or psyche, can take a tremendous amount of pressure, can adapt to a fantastic amount of change, but there is a limit. When an individual is subjected to unrelenting change, it eventually seems that he cannot cope with it. He becomes confused, nervous, and begins to lose his sense of identity. There seems to be nothing permanent to relate to, to hold onto.

For protection from the unrelenting pressures of our environment, we need a spiritual energy field that will absorb the shocks and neutralize the pressures so that we can master our outer environment and use to advantage the wonderful fruits of our knowledge.

This spiritual energy field would certainly help us in the area of communication. We are the best-informed people in history, but this is a rather dubious distinction, because the news media, being in the business of selling newspapers and advertising, often tends to present information in a sensational way. If we are not careful we find ourself reading with our emotions instead of with our mind. We find ourself getting upset over something that "an informed source" or "a source close to the top" has said. (A device sometimes used to give respectability to rumor or gossip.) But in spite of these emotion-arousing and partial-picturing ways of telling what is going on in the world beyond our immediate environment, remember that *one positive thought* will disarm any negative effect on the mind or emotions brought by the day's news.

When you lay down your paper or the radio

news report ends, instead of getting all upset and spinning your emotional wheels, take a moment to bless all the people involved in the news. Take a moment to know there is only one Presence and one Power, God the good omnipotent. Realize that God's harmonizing, peace-producing, miracle-working power is moving in and through all people and events right now. Thus you will conserve your own emotional strength; you will avoid ulcers and high blood pressure; and you will become a stabilizing influence to the whole world.

Another cause of tension and anxiety today is what might be called "symptomatic imaginitis." This simply means that we are bombarded with suggestions of all kinds of possible physical ills, from unsightly dandruff to cancer, and we tend to identify with these suggestions. Our subconscious mind is tremendously sensitive to pictures and suggestions of all kinds. We need to consciously *cancel* the negative suggestions we receive.

When you are exposed to circumstances that could bring on a case of "symptomatic imaginitis," or the tendency to identify with an outer suggestion of illness, say to yourself, "Cancel that! I do not accept it." Then remember that the life within you is perfect life and that your body is biased on the side of health; health is our natural state. Remember the principle: it is what happens *in you*—in your thinking—that determines what will happen *out there* in your body or circumstances.

Even though we have described the present and the immediate future as a threatening environment, the truth is that all this outer change is *good.* We are going through a transitional stage that will lead to a glorious age. Although the world is ready—that is, science is ready, technology is ready—humankind is not yet ready.

We are still trying to escape from our environment in every possible way, and each escape route only leads to more problems, frustration, and degradation of the human spirit. We try drugs, drink, thoughtless divorce, and overeating. We cling to the television and vicariously identify with the heroines and heroes who always master the situation. But escape is never an answer. The coward, the escapist, seems to destroy himself.

The way to real mastery is not finding a way out, but a way *up*—a way to control and master negativity. We need to learn how to set up a spiritual energy field so that we can be shielded from outer pressures and do what needs to be done by us calmly, wisely, and successfully.

First of all, we want to realize that what hurts us, what "drives us up a wall," what makes us impatient, nervous, and afraid is not the changing outer conditions themselves, but our own inner emotional reaction to these conditions. Perhaps we can't change the world and we can't really run away from it. But we certainly can make some change in *us* that will enable us to meet and master our environment and grow in the process.

The only possible right answer lies in the realm of our spiritual nature. In order to tap this spiritual nature, we have first to learn not to react compulsively to outer conditions in a destructively emotional way. As long as these emotional explosions are going on within us, there is no way for our spiritual nature to be heard or to take charge.

How do we do this? How do we *not* get upset when upsetting conditions prevail in our life? How do we *not* get impatient when there are a million things to do, no time to do them, and unexpected delays come up? How do we *not* get irritated at other people who say and do things that annoy us and make us angry? The first step is to look at the outer pressures and challenges in a new light.

We need to see negative conditions not as problems, nerve-racking nuisances, but as valuable, needed, golden opportunities for us to grow, to overcome the compulsive, destructive reaction patterns that prevent our happiness.

It is only through facing again the conditions that have previously upset us, irritated us, even driven us to distraction that we become able to undo the harm that we have allowed them to do. Conditions have no power; *our reaction to them is the only power they can have.* A destructive emotional reaction weakens us. A response free from destructive emotion actually *strengthens* us and gives us mastery, poise, confidence, and strength!

This may sound like bitter medicine—but what we must do is look forward to pressure conditions, to irritating circumstances or people that we may attract into our sphere of living by our own soul's need for growth and overcoming. In a sense, we need to welcome each new opportunity with a will to consciously control our response and purposely refuse to react on negative emotions.

Every time we check that compulsive response, we gain back a little of the power that we have surrendered to outer conditions and people. Each time we take control of our reaction, each time we bridle those "wild horses" of emotion, the energy that we have previously dissipated becomes a spiritual force field around us, making it easier for us to handle the next upsetting encounter in a positive way.

Let's take an example of a destructive emotional response and see how you can convert that energy from a power to hurt you to a power to help you. How about the compulsive emotional response of sarcasm! If you feel that you are being "put down" by other persons, that they are threatening your sense of security, you may compulsively react with a stinging sarcastic put-down of your own. This is hardly a virtue. None of us would go around bragging that we are a sarcastic person, yet many of us are. It is a very common emotional reaction to threats to our ego from other persons or embarrassing circumstances.

The emotional response that surfaces as sarcasm is a corroding agent. It throws the nervous system of the body out of balance, pumping adrenaline into the bloodstream, making the heart beat faster, and doing who-knows-what-other stressful things to the physical being. Then, when the body breaks down in some way from the stress, we innocently cry, "Why do these things happen to me?"

Here is a way to handle a compulsive sarcastic response that you feel so justified in giving in to, but which is destroying you physically and eating away at your awareness of peace. Watch and wait for the very next time a person signals annoyance or a situation occurs in which you feel the temptation to react with a cutting, sarcastic rejoinder. Such a temptation (or opportunity, depending on how you look at it) will come—it has in the past and it surely will again—but this time you will be ready.

You feel that tide of emotion arising, but you are prepared and say to yourself, "Wait, this is *just* the opportunity I have been looking for to assume mastery over my unwanted and destructive emotion." Because you are the boss of your mind and have greater authority than a mere psychological state of anger, fear, guilt, or whatever is prompting the urge to become sarcastic, you smile, stay centered in your spiritual mastery, and silently bless the situation or the person. Remember: *conditions have no power;* your reaction to outer conditions is their only power! A destructive emotional reaction weakens *you.* Conversely, a response free from negative emotion actually strengthens you; it builds a powerful spiritual force field that protects you from the stress of outer change and pressures.

Another cause of tension and nervousness in this present age is what we might call an unfocused mind, the tendency of our thoughts to move quickly from one thing to another, like the flitting of a butterfly. Again, inward control is the answer. Live by the motto, *This one thing I do.* Many successful persons, when asked how they were able to accomplish so much, will reply, "By doing one thing at a time."

The secret is *concentration.* I realize that to many people the word *concentration* brings up thoughts of tension, of gripping something tightly with the mind. But the truth is that concentration is quite the opposite of this. To concentrate means to think about one thing to the exclusion of everything else. When you do this your mind is clear and relaxed.

Try it. Focus your attention on a chair in the room. Just say to yourself: "For the time being, I am just going to mentally examine this chair—to think only about the chair. I will not concern myself with anything else for the next few moments." You will find your mind almost sighing with relief. It doesn't have to worry about or think about anything else but the chair. What a relief!

Of course, you may say, "Well, what about all the other things that need attention in my life? It is one thing to say that I should shut out all other thoughts, but is it realistic?" True, there are many things that need attention in this complex world. But instead of throwing up our hands in dismay, we can use our mind and imagination to fit the principle of relaxed concentration into our "hectic" schedule.

Your mind, your field of consciousness can hold only one conscious thought at a time; and you find that the storage of your previous thoughts can be elusive. You sometimes have to hunt for them when you need them. Here is a suggestion that I have found pleasant and successful: Take a paper and pencil and write down important thoughts—put them right in front of you. If you have to do something else for a while, then when you come back your thoughts are just as you left them, recorded on paper.

Write down the different things you have to and want to do during the day. List the things that are on your mind today. Write on the same paper: "I totally accept the belief that the presence and power of God is working with me to help me to easily, effortlessly, and successfully accomplish what is necessary. I am grateful!"

You will find that writing a statement of Truth evokes a much more powerful response in you than merely "thinking" it. Look over the list and choose the things you most *feel like doing,* and get started. Getting started is much easier this way than to force yourself to do something you don't feel like doing now.

By doing this, you will find that you can *concentrate* on the thing at hand, the job you have decided to do, and then you don't have to think about the other jobs. When you finish the present task, the next one will be waiting, listed on your portable memory pad.

This is another way of adapting principle: It is not what happens to you or around you, but what happens *in* you. Spirituality cannot be separated from everyday life. You would not be living if it weren't for the spiritual life-energy that is enlivening you! It is only when we, in our mind, try to separate the so-called "sacred" from the so-called "secular" that we find ourself alone, helpless, tense, worried, and afraid.

It is not what happens to you or around you that is important. What is important is how you respond. If you respond with the remembrance that the transcendent power and wisdom of God are working with you, for you, and through you, you have found the answer to living life successfully. Carry with you the idea that the little girl was thinking, God is the stabilizing force in me that keeps me right side up—when my world seems upside down!

Succinctly, when you stop thinking and speaking and listing your priorities in an *un*spiritual way, you automatically begin to concentrate your energy in a poised, relaxed, *spiritual* way.

Did you know that when diamonds are mined, they are covered with hard layers of dirt and grime? When these layers are chipped off, the diamond is already there. Similarly, you are a spiritual being, a perfect and beautiful child of God. When you eliminate or chip off all those habitual emotional responses of anger, jealousy, sarcasm, resentment, confusion, and delay, (we all know the list!) you don't put spirituality *in*—you merely reveal the shining Truth that was and is there all the time!

You can't stop what arises in your mind, but you can stop what you allow to remain there.

Get rid of the weeds, and what is left is good grain!

Get rid of the coating of dirt, and what is left is the sparkling diamond!

Get rid of what love is not, and what is left is love!

Get rid of the negative emotional reaction, and what is left is a spiritual response!

Get rid of the distractions and confusion, and what is left is clarity and focus of energy!

Get rid of tension and stress in your thinking and feeling, and what is left is the peace and power of your spiritual reality!

Develop Patience
and a Plan

There is one particular quality of mind essential to spiritual unfoldment. It is admittedly difficult to develop, but without it we make little progress in learning to attune ourself to the beneficent forces and laws of God. This quality is *patience.*

Patience is something you cannot buy. It cannot be inherited. It cannot be given to you in any way. Patience is an attitude of mind that you alone must develop and nourish until it becomes an established, automatic, and effortless response in the face of problems that seem to take endless amounts of time to solve.

Patience is a sign of maturity—both emotional and spiritual. When a two-year-old child can't have his ice cream cone right away, what does he do? He stamps his feet and goes into a tantrum of impatience. An adult who is emotionally immature may be reserved enough to not stamp his feet in a childish way, but when he wants something badly that he can't have right now, he may become bitter and angry. His inner reactions are not much different from the two-year-old's.

Spiritual maturity needs to accompany emotional maturity. The person who is spiritually mature knows that God is never late. The person who is spiritually mature knows that God works through spiritual law and that the operation of divine law is always a *process.*

Jesus points out how all things must come through a process of growth. He says:

> *The kingdom of God is as if a man should scatter seed upon the ground, and should sleep and rise night and day, and the seed should sprout and grow, he knows not how. The earth produces of itself, first the blade, then the ear, then the full grain in the ear—Mark 4:26-28.*

Here very definitely and clearly, Jesus is pointing out that the answer from God to your prayerful request, the fulfillment from God of your legitimate need, comes from the kingdom of God. But as it enters the kingdom of matter or form, it must conform to the law of natural growth.

In other words, your full and complete healing, or the establishment of harmony in a broken human relationship, or whatever the answer to your need or good desire, is essentially a *process.* And a process means that one thing follows the other in an orderly and necessary way.

Just as Jesus pointed out, we see this process clearly in nature, and we accept it with patience. When we plant a seed today we do not expect it to be a full-grown plant tomorrow. But we know that someday it will be a full-grown plant, so we patiently wait—meanwhile watering and caring for it. Yet somehow with our problems and challenges in life, we want and sometimes expect the answer to burst forth immediately.

People who think Truth should work like a magician who shouts, "Abracadabra!" and *poof,* a bouquet of flowers appears or a rabbit pops out—are getting both feet off the ground. We need to have one foot in heaven (the kingdom of God) and one foot on the ground (the formed world). With one foot in heaven we acknowledge the existence of God and His ability to help us in every need. But with the other foot on earth, we realize that the translation of the answer from the kingdom of the unformed to the kingdom of the formed requires a process that involves the factor of *time.* As Jesus said, "First the blade, then the ear, then the full grain in the ear."

Let me hasten to add here that the time factor in translating the perfect answer that exists *now* in the kingdom of God into the formed answer of our physical world can be speeded up! I am not unaware that there have been instantaneous healings; but by instantaneous, we realize that the healing *process*—already begun—was tremendously accelerated and completed.

The time factor has to do with our consciousness. By that I mean, the more we can keep our faith centered on and in God, the more we can eliminate doubt, fear, and all negative mental states from our consciousness, thus, the more rapidly this process takes place.

When we work with Truth, with God, we can never really lose! For the longer our faith is tested, the stronger it grows. Even though our answer may seem long in coming, when it *does* appear the pain and inconvenience will soon be forgotten. But the tremendous consciousness of faith in God that we develop will be ours forever and it will make subsequent challenges and problems much easier to handle.

In addition, the trying of our faith invariably brings the priceless gift of understanding, the gaining of which is more to be valued, testified Solomon, than silver or gold—for understanding is the active *cause* of all that we call good.

When we are impatient, we are really working against ourself, for impatience, as you well know from personal experience, is definitely a negative and destructive attitude of mind. We say, "He was fuming with impatience!" or, "I got sick and tired of waiting!" Believe me, these are not just meaningless metaphors!

Impatience does "burn us up" physically and make the chemistry of our body "fume." Impatience actually does make us sick and tired. With this destructive mental attitude storming through our field of consciousness, the power of God is short-circuited in us and the time factor for our answer to come from the everywhere-present kingdom of God into this four-dimensional world of length, width, depth, and time, is expanded.

Impatience denotes a lack of faith. There are two kinds of impatience. One is the kind where we wish with all our heart that the seed we planted would hurry up and develop into the stalk of corn we so greatly desire. But we know that there is a necessary process involved, so we busy ourself with other things and the impatience subsides. The other kind of impatience is the kind that gets us so distraught and nervous and jumpy that the first thing we know we are digging up the seed to see if it is growing. We have doubts about the outcome, otherwise we wouldn't dig up the seed to see! This is the kind of impatience that we want to overcome. This is the impatience that reveals a shallow faith. Our religion is *what we believe to be true.* If we really believe it is true that God is all-powerful and all-wise, loves us, and is working with us, then although we may experience little pangs of impatience (wishing the goal were accomplished), in a deeper sense we are at peace and willing to let God work things out in His perfect way.

Sometimes we become impatient because we

cannot see how some present experience can possibly be a part of the answer to our problem. Here again is where faith and patience enter in. When this happens in my life I am reminded of a picture puzzle I saw in a magazine years ago. It contained magnified pictures of portions of familiar objects—such as a fork or a thimble. When I saw the greatly magnified small portion of the object, it looked threatening. I wondered what awful machine this could be a part of! But I remember the embarrassed feeling I had when I turned to the answer page and saw that the puzzle pieces were only the tine of a fork, a portion of a cabbage grater.

Life is like that. Sometimes we are so immersed in the present moment that it appears to be a blown-up portion of the overall answer to our problem. This small, but greatly enlarged portion looks like anything but good. But if we could see the *whole* picture in perspective, or if we can have the faith to know that the whole picture is good (even though the part we are looking at and experiencing presently doesn't appear to be good) then we can lean back mentally and know that everything truly *is* in divine order, having the faith and patience to know that God knows what He is doing! As we do this, we help to accelerate the time factor and hasten the manifestation of our good.

Many of Charles Fillmore's thoughts are

recorded in a little book called *The Revealing Word,* a dictionary of words commonly found in Truth articles. Under the word *patience* we read: "An attitude of mind characterized by poise, inner calmness, and quiet endurance, especially in the face of trying conditions. Patience has its foundation in faith, and it is perfected only in those who have unwavering faith in God."

"The proving of your faith worketh patience"—James 1:3.

Whatever worldly problems you are facing today, your perfect answer exists now in the "other" world—the kingdom of God. The kingdom of God isn't an after-death place. It is, as Jesus taught, at hand—even within you. The kingdom of God exists simultaneously with this physical world. But to get your answer from the unformed world, the kingdom of God, into your formed world, there is a process involving time. So be patient. Busy yourself with what is at hand to do. Trust—don't doubt.

God is never late. Meanwhile, keep giving thanks to God for the perfect fulfillment under divine timing, for gratitude is a spiritual catalyst that speeds up the process of converting spiritual substance into form.

Most of us acknowledge the Truth that there is a transcendent Power and Intelligence, powerful enough to bring the unformed answers to prayer into the world of the formed. Most of us acknowledge that this transcendent Power and Intelligence is not a kingly figure on a throne in the sky; rather, it is an invisible Presence which fills all space and which indwells each person as the animated spark, the very life of the individual.

The big question is how to consciously attune ourself to the activity of this everywhere-present, transcendent Power and Presence that we call God. Let's explore such a method or technique. I can only impart it to you as an idea; you must take that idea and specialize it or adapt it in your own individual way.

Here are the key words to this dynamic idea: *patience and a plan.* Let's begin our explanation of this idea by observing once again the principle of patience and a plan in nature. We can learn much about the laws and principles of God by studying the simple, uncomplicated movements of nature.

Imagine that you are kneeling on the ground in your garden. You have just finished spading the ground. You have made sure your row would be straight by placing a twig at either end and drawing a string from one twig to another. You have tilted your hoe sideways and made a furrow along the string. And now you are kneeling alongside the furrow with a brightly colored package of radish seeds in your hand. You take one small radish seed, place it in your hand, and look at it. It is just a hard brown speck; but if you take time to think about it, you know you are looking at a potential miracle. Look again at this tiny seed in your palm. Within that seed is the pattern of a radish; within that seed is both the intelligence and the means to develop it into a beautiful red radish with large, intricately formed leaves.

How is it done? Nobody knows, not even the radish. But the radish doesn't have to know how it is done. Neither do you, the planter, need to know how it is done. All the radish needs, all you need, is *patience and a plan.* In the case of a radish, the plan is enfolded in the seed; it is invisible. You can take the seed apart and discover no blueprint. It is an idea; but the plan is there. Plant the seed and have patience, and you will see the outer replica of the invisible plan come forth.

Whatever problem is causing you anxiety, whatever desire is burning within you, apply this principle of patience and a plan! The plan is a mental blueprint. You think of your problem-condition or desire; next you "insert" the mental blueprint in it, and then you "plant" the activated seed in God-Mind. That is, you give it to God!

For instance, what is the problem or deep desire? Is it for healing? Is it for happier and more fulfilling human relationships? Is it for supply to meet a legitimate need? Say to yourself, "This is the way things are, right now. I don't like them. I don't completely understand how or why this came about. But I *do* know that these limited conditions are not God's will for me. God's will for me and for all concerned is *always* in the direction of increasing health, happiness, success, and abundance of good for His highest creation—mankind. So, following the simplest principle of growth and unfoldment, I must formulate a plan for God—for this Principle of increase of good—to work through."

Here is how you formulate the invisible plan which God will eventually bring into form and into your experience. Say your problem is that of healing. Here is the plan that you can formulate. See yourself whole and well, vibrant and vital. This, you agree in your heart, is logically and truly God's will for you. How could it be other than your heavenly Father's will for you, His beloved child! See yourself whole and well, vibrant and vital! Hold this vision. Know in the deepest part of your being that this plan, this vision, is potentially possible—for the transcendent power and intelligence of God is capable of doing all things. And then—patience. You don't know just *how* this is going to come about, but you know in your heart that it is. You recognize that all healing is a process, both physical and mental. Things in your body need to be rearranged and in a certain order; but, certain things—beliefs, subconscious blocks—must also be rearranged in or eliminated from your mind, which includes the vast subconscious. This takes place as an orderly process—one thing necessarily preceding the next.

How this is going to be done, you don't know; and in a sense you don't care. You do know this transcendent Power and Intelligence can and will unfold the plan for your health in the divinely right and perfect way. Meanwhile you live each moment as it comes, looking for the good in it, looking for opportunities to give, ever seeking to see how you can express more of God's qualities of joy, beauty, life, and creativity in whatever condition you are presently living—knowing all the time that God's will of increasing health is moving through you toward the fulfillment of the invisible plan of a totally healthy body.

Step by step, you will be led into those circumstances or experiences that are sequentially a part of the orderly process of the unfoldment of your answer. Conditions do not just happen—they grow; just as a flower grows from seed to full bloom. Answers grow from an idea or plan by an orderly process toward outer fulfillment.

You can follow the same principle as described here for prosperity, or for a human relations problem, or for any other challenge. For instance, know that it is God's will that you be serene and happy. See and feel yourself supremely happy. Don't try to picture the circumstances of your happiness—just feel how you would feel if you were supremely happy. Know that this *is* possible.

Are not all things possible to this almighty Power that Jesus revealed as your Father?

Sure, the present facts may be discouraging. Perhaps you are separated from a loved one or feel that someone hates you and there seems to be no way to change the inflexible and impossible conditions you are in. But forget about the means. Leave them to God.

Have patience and a plan. Know that good and happiness beyond your present imagination are in the making for you. Give heartfelt thanks for the joyous outcome, knowing that it is just as inevitable as the coming of spring each year. Meanwhile, live each moment deeply, richly, looking for the beauty and goodness there. Soon the plan will start to show. Just a little will show at first; perhaps like the tiny rootlets that feel their way out from the seed. Take one step at a time—the step at hand. Rejoice in these rootlets of your good, for they are the prophecy of the good that is to come.

You may think that this is just a lot of "Pollyanna" theory. The present facts of your life will be so glaringly obvious and seemingly unyielding at times. However, there is more to this world than what we perceive with our senses. There is an invisible *something* which is ever moving toward the increase of good, of life, of beauty, of abundance. It takes an act of faith and courage to step out of the fascination of present conditions and to mold the future with what seems like little more than a dream. Have the faith and courage to try. Remember, that invisible plan in the radish seed has no more substance than a dream, yet you know that with patience its dream will come true.

There is a principle of harmony that stands behind all music. A musical score is not music, it is the *plan.* You place the musical score on your music stand and you attempt to get in tune with the principle of harmony that lies within it. At first you may not be very much in tune with the principle of harmony in the music, but each time you practice you get a little closer to that perfect harmony, and each time you improve, you feel a thrill of accomplishment, even though you may be far from a Carnegie Hall candidate.

Make your plan for health, for unfailing prosperity, for lasting happiness. Moment by moment, live in a consciousness of God's presence and power and soon you will be in perfect tune with the principle of good, effortlessly and beautifully living the plan.

Patience and a plan—the dynamo is in the word *patience.* Faith is patience. Patience is waiting, and while you are waiting, living. It is living completely in the present moment, drinking of the good that is in it, while in the back of your mind you gratefully know that increasing good is on its way.

Find Your Purpose

What is the purpose of life? There must be greater purpose than what we see happening to us and to others. People often seem to find their whole purpose in the pattern of growing up physically, going to school, getting a job, falling in love, getting married, having children, saving for the children's education, planning retirement, and then, hopefully, dying easily without much pain or trouble to the family.

If we can do all these things successfully, we feel we have lived a good life. But what is it good *for?* It seems like a lifelong obstacle course, considering all the challenges one must face along the way. What is the reward for successful completion of this life cycle? Years ago in Sunday school, I was told that the reward was going to a wonderful place called "heaven" where there would be no more hardship, no more lack, no more sickness, and where everyone would be equal.

This story of life's ultimate purpose sufficed for me until I got old enough to ask questions and read the Bible for myself without the Sunday-school teacher or minister telling me what it was *supposed* to mean. It seemed to me that Jesus never talked about these wonderful things as if they were in the great "by-and-by" after death. He talked about the here and now! He taught that the kingdom of God is at hand—even within us. I decided that whatever the purpose of life is, it must be something that is found in the here and now—something far greater than the weary cycle we so often see.

A good starting place in our quest for true purpose is the *mind*. Just as life must have a greater purpose than the outer cradle-to-grave, sequential events, so must this mind of ours have a greater purpose than to plan the day's duties, or to store information from books, or to calculate how to make a larger profit at business.

Our emotions make up an important facet of what we loosely term "the mind." Our emotions seem to lie in us like a huge, ultra-sensitive field. When something pleasurable is reflected through any of the five outer senses, the sensitive emotional field makes us happily excited. When something irritating, upsetting, or threatening is encountered by any of the outer senses, the super-sensitive emotional field excites us with a flare of anger, avoidance, or hatred.

71

This is what we have to work with; this is our outer life, passing moment-by-moment, hour-by-hour. Our mind watches the outer parade while our emotions compulsively respond to what we see, perhaps the way the old player pianos responded to the holes punched in a roll of music.

I don't know the whole answer; as I once heard someone say, "I'm just beginning to know the questions!" However, I feel that the path to the answer lies in the idea of growth, unfoldment. We are living entities and the nature of a living thing is to grow. What is there to grow in us? Certainly the physical body grows and develops for eighteen years or so. But then what else grows? We may enlarge our store of information through study and experience. We may broaden our awareness by the mere fact of staying alive.

New Thought teaches that what grows or is capable of growth in us is the seed-idea of perfect Being, which is enfolded in every person by the Creator of all things. Even as the idea, the invisible pattern of a complete oak tree is enfolded in an acorn (and not only the pattern of the complete oak tree is there, but also all the plans and directions for the complicated development from the first tiny rootlet, through the sapling stage, to the final complete expression), in human beings is enfolded the pattern and the plan for the ultimate, full, and complete expression of God's perfect idea of Being.

We call this perfect idea that God has enfolded in each person *the Christ*. Paul referred to it in writing of "the mystery hidden for the ages and generations . . . Christ in you, the hope of glory"—Col. 1:26, 27. Jesus taught this concept of our inner growth, of the unfoldment of that perfect idea that had been divinely enfolded, through a parable. John quotes Jesus as saying, "Truly, truly, I say to you, unless a grain of wheat falls into the earth and dies, it remains alone; but if it dies, it bears much fruit"—John 12:24.

Paul Tillich, a theologian respected by many denominations, used a very descriptive and revealing term for God. He referred to God as the "Ground of Being." This term can help us to understand the parable Jesus has given us. Can you begin to see the principle that the parable is pointing to? You are the grain of wheat. You inherently contain, invisibly within you, the potential for glorious growth into the fulfillment of what you are intended to be. God is the "Ground of Being" in which you are already planted. "In him we live and move and have our being"—Acts 17:28.

The important element here is the "dying." Jesus says that unless the seed dies, it remains alone; but if it dies it grows and in time bears much fruit. This process does not, of course, refer to the death of the body; it refers to the death of the personal ego, the little self, the vain and arrogant state of mind that thinks there is nothing superior to it, that chooses estrangement from God and prefers to go its own willful way with the limited intellect as its prime minister.

The story of the prodigal son is another parable that says the same thing. The prodigal represents the little self, the vain state of mind that insists on going it alone, figuring out intellectually how to handle life successfully. The prodigal was an intelligent person, and he had a lot of money, but what happened to him is a dramatic description of what often happens to us when we choose that path: we become empty, forlorn, miserable, unhappy. As Jesus said in the grain of wheat parable, "it remains alone." That can be a terrifying state—*alone.*

The little self must die, give up its throne, its absolute authority, so that the perfect idea, the Christ, can begin to emerge and grow. The answer is for the prodigal (the arrogant, little self who says in effect, "I want to do it myself, Father") to recognize its own limitations, swallow its pride, and return to obedience to the Father within.

The parable of the prodigal son is a profoundly spiritual teaching. Yet it is commonly thought of as a moral teaching only. We equate the prodigal son with a crook, a weakling, a lazy youth—with anyone of loose or questionable behavior. It might come as a shock to many ministers and good, honest, upright citizens to think of *themselves* as

74

prodigal sons. And yet, there is a sense in which we all are. Some of us may be on our way back to the Father's house—or trying to find our way—but the journey is neither easy nor quick for most of us.

When a grain of wheat falls into the earth and dies, it begins to send little rootlets into the earth around it. If I am the symbolic grain of wheat, when I begin to "come to myself" and at least *desire* to let myself be directed from within, to at least become aware of this state of mind in me that is so vain, selfish, and limited, then I am sending out those little rootlets into the "Ground of Being." They bring the needed nourishment for the God-idea, the Christ in me, to grow, unfold, and express through me and as me.

This dying of the little self isn't easy. In the "little self" state of mind, we have looked to and depended upon outer events, conditions, and people for our good, our happiness, our success. When outer things haven't worked out the way we have wanted them to, we have often blamed them or our own lack of proper planning in the outer realm. Our whole life and fortune may have revolved around outer circumstances and our limited ability to manipulate them successfully to our own advantage. To make a one-hundred-and-eighty degree turn and totally depend upon an invisible Power, a voiceless Guidance, an unseen Presence is not always easy.

Ultimately the growth process, which is the purpose of the spiritual being that you are, comes down to this: on what do you depend? Do you depend on outer circumstances, events, people? Or do you depend on that universal Presence and Power that man calls God, whose kingdom of divine ideas is within you?

If you depend on your job for your comfortable existence, you are its slave and it is your master. A threat of layoffs gives you sleepless nights; a demotion or being passed by for a better position is a disaster. Of course, under this system *you* can become a master, too. If you can manipulate someone into depending on *you*, then he is your slave and you are the master. Watch the greatest game of life. Everyone seems to be trying to become master—through accumulating money or power of some kind—and at the same time we are forced to be dependent on others in order to attain that power.

We do need outer things and people; we should not be dependent upon them. When we depend on God, our needs are fulfilled in ways that leave no sense of bondage and they work for the greater good of all concerned, bringing always freedom, light, and peace.

Where does one start on this spiritual journey of independence and true purpose? One starts with meditation. Not meditation to relax. Not meditation to make us more efficient at our work of striving for power and outer success. Not meditation as a new thrill because the previous excitement has worn out its ability to stimulate us. Instead, we need to practice meditation just to "hunger and thirst" after understanding and wisdom. We need to meditate to observe objectively what we are and what we can become. And then, without shame or guilt (for these are just ways of making us think we are paying for our mistakes so that we don't really have to change) we *do* what the inner light makes crystal clear for us to do. Our purpose in life will unfold for us and through us according to divine plan.

The practice of meditation and spiritual "self-analysis" helps us to find and to fulfill our real purpose in life, and to answer that persistent questioning, that wondering, "What is the purpose of it all?" We need the assurance and guidance of meditation to satisfy this longing, especially when we go through a period when one hard challenge after another hits us.

I remember talking with a man several years ago who was hitting bottom—physically, emotionally, and spiritually. His wife had divorced him. Because of the emotional strain at home before and during the divorce, he had let his small business go downhill. Several months previously he had an auto accident and although it was not entirely his fault, there were all kinds of legal complications still unsolved. His health, because of all this tension, was not good. "What is the purpose of it all?" he asked. "You work, you try, but it is as if life has something against you."

I could certainly understand his discouraged viewpoint and I tried to help. The essence of what I told him is: *The purpose of life and living is to continually find ways of allowing God to express through us as some form of good—beauty, wholeness, order, prosperity, love, harmony, peace—whatever good is needed at our present place in life.*

I told my friend to discard the concept of God as a "person," an individual somewhere in the sky who has personal control over all the events in each person's life, an individual that, through prayer, could be prevailed upon to change things for us a little bit here and a little bit there.

Jesus opened the door to a new concept when He described God as Spirit, everywhere-present Spirit. Try to catch this vision of God as an invisible, but ever-present creative Energy and Wisdom. All things must have a cause. Nothing just happens; something caused everything. We think of this invisible creative Energy and Wisdom as *First Cause.*

In the beginning this universal creative Energy caused itself to come forth into individual modes of expression: solar systems, planets, water, land, vegetation, animal life, and, as its highest creation, human beings. Let's really try to catch the wholeness of this vision. We look around us at what we call nature: the trees, mountains, stars, and wild life are all modes of expression of the one invisible, universal, creative life Energy. Where do we fit in? We, too, are points of expression of this vast, fathering or originating Spirit, but with a difference. God's highest creation has the power to think, to understand, and therefore, the power to recognize his Source. We have the innate ability to work with that Source in bringing forth increasingly greater good.

This is our greatest purpose in life—to learn to make of ourself an evermore perfect channel for God, the underlying creative life Force, to work through. God needs us! That is why universal Spirit created us. If God didn't need us, there would be no reason for us to be here. God made us in His image and after His likeness. Universal Spirit has an instrument in us through which to find greater expression of itself as love, order, beauty, life—all good.

Now, let's consider how all this relates to your life and problems today. Once you catch the idea that God needs you in order to get into expression as greater good, then your life with its problems takes on an entirely different look. Take, for instance, the man we spoke about earlier who had all sorts of trouble—family, business, legal, and health. He had the opportunity to allow the one creative Power to express through him to establish order, harmony, wholeness, and happiness.

Can it be done in your life? Of course it can! Nothing is impossible to the creative Power of the universe. It all depends on setting up the right mental conditions so that the Power can work through you. How do you do it? The first step is to stop looking to the outer environment—people, organizations, books, economic conditions, lucky breaks, and all the rest—for guidance, good, rewards, or purpose. Instead, begin to train yourself to look to God, to the light of Truth, the light of wisdom within!

Transfer your present dependency on friends, parents, job, education, seniority, stock portfolio, or anything else, to God; not to a God in the sky, but to God as the Spirit of light, wisdom, infinite potentiality within *you.* The very fact that people become so discouraged when things go wrong in the outer is incontrovertible evidence that their faith and dependency have been on things, people, conditions, rather than on God.

It is easy for the personal ego to say, "I love God, I have faith in God, I depend on God," when everything is going smoothly in the outer. The confrontation between "lip service" and honest faith comes when the sturdy-appearing facade of outer conditions starts crumbling at our feet!

I suggest that you pause right here and seriously think about the degree to which you depend upon outer conditions, possessions, and people.

You might find, if you are completely honest, that although you had considered yourself a God-believer all your life, had faithfully attended church and studied the Bible and religious books, that somehow you have missed the biggest point.

You might find that if some of the things you now enjoy and depend on were taken away or even changed to some degree, you would feel crushed, angry, forsaken, helpless, thus proving that your love, faith, and dependency are actually centered in outer things and not in the inner presence and power of God. Be thankful for that insight, for it is the first step toward a realistic faith in God, the unseen but very real Power behind the apparent environmental world.

Coming to this realization, you will then understand that your mental attitudes have everything to do with allowing God's help, wisdom, and infinite resources to come through you to enrich your inner and outer life. For your inner attitudes—over which you have control—either block or facilitate the activity and expression of God through you.

You will learn to understand that your only enemies are of your own mental household. These enemies are your negative emotional reactions to the events, people, and conditions in your life. They are your enemies, because an emotional reaction of anger, fear, irritation, resentment, or impatience has effectively and uncompromisingly cut off the flow of God-power and God-wisdom through you.

In addition to watching your inward response to outer conditions and practicing responding with patience and calmness, you will also want to spend more time getting acquainted with your new Source of dependency—God. Meditation will buoy you up during the "questioning times," for it is the process by which you get acquainted with God within you. In time you will deepen that acquaintance to the intimacy of oneness.

Previously when your dependency was on outer things and people, you spent a lot of time thinking about them, didn't you? You worried about your job. You became lost in thought trying to figure out why some person seemed to be avoiding you. If you are switching your dependency (which means your faith) to God, you will spend that worry-time and lost-in-thought time going within to let the light of understanding permeate your mind, to absorb the light as a plant absorbs the sun.

In summation, my answer to the discouraged is this:

God needs us; why else would He create us in His image and likeness? Animals with bodies such as ours would have served the purpose of populating the planet, were that the only reason for our creation. But we are created with the unique gift of self-consciousness and the power of free choice. We have the potential equipment, the inherent (although often latent) ability to be a channel through which God can express fully as increasing life, love, beauty, growth, and joy, toward the fulfillment of the divine plan.

In order to understand, enjoy, and fulfill your own unique purpose, you have to depend solely on God—not on outer things or people—and look forward to the so-called outer challenges or problems as opportunities to grow, to unfold that Christ potential, to prove your ultimate and intimate dependency on God. The promise is, the assurance is, God will never let you down. His beautiful purpose for you is now unfolding!

Hasten Your Healing!

"The Importance of the Will to Live!" is the title of an article that once appeared in the magazine section of an Indianapolis Sunday paper. It was written by Henry Huber, MD, a surgeon for a New York hospital. Dr. Huber wrote: "It is important for everyone to understand that even today in this era of wonder drugs and miracle operations, your attitude, cooperation, and acceptance of an *active role* are of the utmost importance in getting back on your feet. Some patients have the mistaken impression that their role can be purely passive—[that] all they have to do is stay in bed, take the medication prescribed, and all will be well. Nothing can be further from the truth!"

It is exciting, amazing, and satisfying, to hear a medical doctor publicly agree with and validate a teaching that New Thought has emphasized for many years—that the mind, its thinking, and its attitude are decisive factors in healing! But it is one thing to make a statement that strikes home as true and valid, and it is another thing to put the theory into practical use. In short, how do we do it?

The cooperation that we can give in the healing process is not wholly physical in nature, but also mental and spiritual; it involves prayer and faith. But how do we pray? On what do we anchor our faith?

We begin to see that our "active role" in the healing process requires a certain amount of skill and learning on our part, just as the surgeon's active role requires skill and learning. The important element to be activated is *faith.* There are two kinds of faith: blind faith and understanding faith.

Blind faith works very well up to a point. But when appearances seem to get worse instead of better, the icy grip of fear may begin to snuff out the candle of blind faith. Then we may find the high-sounding statements about "active roles" and "right attitudes" rather empty. They make good parlor talk, but in the grip of a fever or surrounded by the confining walls of a hospital room, they may turn to ashes on the tongue.

Understanding faith stands the test of threatening appearances. Even though cold mists of fear may arise from time to time, the flame of understanding faith is not extinguished, and eventually it dissipates the mists of fear.

Unlike understanding faith, blind faith is usually based on a three-letter word, rather than a transcendent, yet indwelling Presence. That word is *God.* The word actually means *good;* it is a fine word to use to describe the universal creative Power and Intelligence. But unless we have some idea of what the word stands for, we are limited in our understanding. The true meaning of the word *God* is not the anthropomorphic concept of the term, a concept of God as being in the form and nature of a human being. To many people the word *God* means a bearded Man on a throne of some sort in the sky. There He abides in all His power and authority, watching over us humans on the planet earth as we scramble around trying to make a living, trying to find people or circumstances that will make us happy.

But when an individual with this limited concept of God becomes feverish, afraid, his first thought may be to try to get God's attention through prayer. Thus he pleads and begs; he may strive to reason with God, feeling that if God is as loving as he has been taught, then He must feel sorry for him in his awful plight and turn His attention toward him.

If there are no immediate results from this kind of prayer, then the individual may go a step further and bargain. He will promise, perhaps, to go to church regularly, or to give more to the church, or to do volunteer work for the needy, or to give up some personal pleasure, if only God will listen and grant his request. Some persons even seem to be trying to impress God by keeping a Bible handy in the house, or by displaying religious pictures or statues. These are beautiful tools and symbols of spiritual devotion and unfoldment, but without deep spiritual feeling, they are of little value in getting results.

But underneath all the bargaining, pleading, and outer ritual, the individual may still have an empty feeling. His real faith is in the outer—in the effectiveness of a certain miracle drug, in some looked-for outcome, or in what he hopes is the omnipotent wisdom of the doctor.

I have heard people say that they feel some doctors act as if they were "little gods." More often, the case is that people in their desperation place the doctor in that unenviable role. Most doctors are well aware of their human limitations and realize their dependence on the mysterious and seemingly unpredictable life force that is innate in the patient.

Understanding faith involves a knowledge of and an attunement with the divine life force within us. Understanding faith is neither discouraged nor extinguished. Understanding faith is based on the rock of Truth and knows that what is true is eternally and unchangeably true. Outer conditions and the passage of time do not alter the Truth.

What is this unalterable, unchanging eternal Truth? It is that God is Spirit, as Jesus taught. The word *spirit* comes from the Latin word *spiritus,* which means "breath." God is the very breath of life. The word *respiration* has the same root. Breath is the symbol and indicator of life. So it is easy to understand God the Spirit as being the universal life of which all things are individualized expressions.

The breath of life is not merely the breathing apparatus in the physical body; but it is the spark of conscious awareness in us. This spark of consciousness in us is what makes us what we are. It is the awareness of ourself as a living, unique being that is best described when we say, "I am!" God, as the universal life force, is the source of the life which we call "our life" and which in its pure and natural state is the healing power of the universe.

This is the bridge, the relationship between God and us. God is the universal Spirit that we experience as our basic conscious awareness, our "I am." This universal life force that lives in and through each of us is the power that heals. In reality, spiritual healing is the only kind of healing there is.

Doctors may bandage, treat, manipulate, and prescribe helpful substances and conditions, but then they can only wait for "nature" to take over and do the actual healing. Their work doesn't heal, it provides a more favorable climate for the healing, restorative process to renew and strengthen the body to its normal operation. Whether we call this invisible, intangible, but very real healing power nature, or life force, or Spirit, makes little difference. All of us must admit its existence and its universality—its presence and activity at all times in all persons.

But when we use the term spiritual healing, we specifically associate healing with prayer, and prayer is associated with the activity of the mind. Just as the physician bandages, treats, prescribes, or adjusts for the purpose of providing the most favorable conditions for the healing power to take over and complete the restoration to normalcy, so does one who prays or who practices spiritual healing seek to provide the most favorable conditions of mind so that the divine healing power can flow fully and swiftly to restore the body to wholeness.

The wise doctor acknowledges, even depends on this healing, restorative tendency innate to the very cells and organs of the body. Every cell of the body has a very strong "will to live" and can only be weakened when conditions become unfavorable. However, it is not a part of the cell's work to question or investigate from where this very real and obvious inner tendency comes. The Truth student, or one who studies and practices spiritual healing, is very interested in where this healing tendency, this universal life force comes from and what mental conditions encourage its increasingly powerful expression. The logical premise is that the connecting point between God and the individual is the human mind.

Where else could the connecting point be? There must be a connecting point or we would not be alive. The connecting point is not the heart or any other part of the body, not even the brain. The brain is a physical, cellular instrument for the expression of that spiritual thing called the *mind!* The student of spiritual healing concludes that to provide the most favorable conditions of mind enables the universal life energy to flow without obstruction, thereby accelerating the healing process.

It is easy to see, then, that the doctor and the one who practices spiritual prayer are not working against each other, but with each other. Both acknowledge the one Source of the healing power; even though one may call it nature, and the other, God. The doctor seeks to provide the most favorable conditions in the physical body; the prayer seeks to provide the most favorable conditions of mind for the one Power to do its perfect healing work.

More and more, doctors are beginning to acknowledge that the mind has an important role in the healthy flow of the life force. Research has indicated that continually tense and anxious individuals seem to become physically ill more often and more seriously than individuals who are nor-

90

mally calm and confident, who are not subject to compulsive emotional reactions, who are slow to anger. The conclusion is that those whose minds are usually flooded with destructive emotions seem to experience more physical illness than those who have learned to remain emotionally tranquil.

The student of spiritual healing says, "Amen!" to that. For decades New Thought has been teaching the necessity of avoiding thoughts and feelings of anger, hatred, unforgiveness, fear, and tension, if we want to keep the mind-channel clear for the Spirit of God to flow through us to renew, restore, revitalize, and heal the physical body.

Myrtle Fillmore, the cofounder of Unity, found healing by "talking" to her body. She relates how very ill she was and that the doctors and medicines had ceased to give her relief. She writes: "I told the life in my liver that it was not torpid or inert, but full of vigor and energy." Then she explains how she spoke similar words to all of the apparently afflicted organs and life centers of her body. She carefully watched her words and thoughts, allowing no negative thought or destructive emotion to remain any longer than it took to sweep it out of her mind. Yes, she was healed completely! It was her seemingly miraculous healing that inspired her husband Charles Fillmore to believe—and thus the Unity movement was born.

A miracle of healing? Yes. But we see miracle healings as a result of the knowledge and skill of chiropractors, osteopaths, and doctors, too. In every instance, the favorable conditions for the one life energy to express were provided—in the mind, or in the body, or in both.

We have learned, then, that one specific way to implement healing is to *talk* to the body, to bless it. Our body is intelligent. It responds to the power of our loving word. We should never, never curse our body, saying things like, "this blasted back of mine," or "my weak stomach." The body will respond to these words, too, but in an undesirable way!

Another specific spiritual healing treatment is the use of affirmations. An affirmation is a statement of belief, as opposed to the apparent facts. For instance, the apparent fact may be that you have a cold, a headache, a fever, or the flu. The thermometer may testify to a high temperature in your body, and the pain may testify with an urgency that cannot be denied; those are the facts. Now consider the Truth, what we might call the "spiritual facts." The Truth is that you are a child of God, a spiritual being. You are a point of expression of the one universal Spirit of God. The spiritual fact is that God as life energy is flowing to and through you at this moment and in every moment to revitalize and heal you.

In affirmative healing prayer, we take our atten-

92

tion off the outer facts and place it on the Truth. This does not mean that we deny that the outer facts exist; it merely means that we are mentally dwelling on the unchanging spiritual Truth. A healing prayer statement to use is: *God is with me. His life is strong in me. He is healing and perfecting me now. I am grateful!*

This is the Truth. Affirm the Truth in spite of the facts, even in the very face of the facts. This provides the right conditions of mind for the universal healing power to come through. The first thing you know, the "facts" begin to change. The Truth does not change; it is the same, whether your body expresses sickness or health. Now you begin to be attuned with that wholeness that is the Truth of your being, and the outpicturing of health is natural and sure.

Affirm for yourself: *God is with me. God's life is strong in me. God's life in me is ever moving toward the increase of livingness, health, and perfection!* And give thanks in advance for the healing that is already yours in Spirit.

An acknowledgment of this Bible-based Truth is the rock upon which understanding faith is built. Our purpose in prayer and meditation is *not* to change a physical condition, but more vividly and completely to experience our oneness with the universal life force. Understanding faith is based also on the premise that God as Spirit is not only the life force, but also the infinite intelligence of the universe. To the extent that we can rid ourself of accumulated limited and false beliefs about the power of appearances and instead tie our faith to the primacy of God's power and presence, we truly realize that infinite intelligence is working through every element of our life toward one end—our ultimate healing.

What this means for us in real results is that we begin to relax, let go, and *let God.* We place God in charge of our healing. Just as each person's fingerprints are individual, so is each body temple a completely unique entity. What or who can supervise our own individual process of healing better than God's infinite intelligence?

We usually try to catalog and categorize illnesses. But the fact is that there are no two bodies physiologically the same, so there are no two physical conditions exactly the same. It just makes good common sense to depend on the universal Physician with infinite wisdom to supervise the intricate process of our personal healing.

Once we become acquainted and find agreement with these basic spiritual principles, we are in a position to really play an "active role" in our healing. There is a time for a thermometer to be placed under our tongue, for tests to be made, for treatment to be worked out for us. But there is also a time for us to get still, to pray with understanding, and to feel the surge of universal life rushing through our point of connection with God.

Remember, one with blind faith is prone to plead, to beg, and to try to get God's attention and sympathy. Understanding faith realizes that there is no need to get God's attention. God is always closer to us even than our breathing. God already knows all about our challenge, and we already have His attention. We don't have to beg and bargain. We only have to "Be still, and know that I am God"—Psalms 46:10.

"Be still." You are not going anywhere. Rest in Spirit. Be still in your mind. Stop those racing thoughts of impatience and self-pity; stop those "injured innocence" thoughts, such as: Why me? What did I do to deserve this? Be still, be still. Be patient, but firm, with yourself. Give yourself time to settle down inwardly.

You may find it helpful at this point to work with the Lord's Prayer. Work with it, do not just repeat it. This prayer is so familiar to us that it is possible to say or think its words while at the same time our thoughts are running around in pandemonium backstage. Instead, as you speak or think the words, seek to realize what they mean. When you come to the words, "give us this day our daily bread," consider that this does not mean material needs exclusively; if your body is in a condition of stress, "bread" means the very *substance* of energy, life, and health.

When you are still and calm, you might use

statements such as these to break up the doubts in your mind:

I am more than my body. I am a spiritual being. I am an emanation, an expression, an individualization of the eternal, universal Spirit of God. The healing, renewing, adjusting universal life force is moving through me now. I feel it. I welcome it. I surrender my personal will to it. I am at peace, I am whole, I am grateful!

Then, no matter whether or not there is a change in the outer, cling to this unchanging Truth. The physical part of your healing may have to do with physicians and changing conditions. But the spiritual phase of your healing does not have to do with these facts; your focus is on the changeless Truth. The outer facts will change. A fever, a bruise, a headache are facts. They change from hour to hour. But God's presence within you as the life of your life, as the healing, strengthening power, is much more than a fact; it is the Truth. This Truth doesn't change from hour to hour, nor from year to year. It is true eternally.

Slowly but surely more and more members of the healing professions are coming to see the importance of the upliftment of mind in the healing process. Now we often find bright and colorful, uplifting hospital surroundings, relaxing music piped in, all sorts of things being done to help the patients to be relaxed, calm, serene, and positive—the exact mental conditions that practitioners of spiritual healing have always said were necessary.

Every day, every year, the healing sciences of medicine, osteopathy, and chiropractic are getting closer and closer to the science of religion. Centuries ago the doctor and the priest were one and the same person. Today we may be too specialized for that to happen, but we are getting progressively closer to the teamwork that utilizes both the divine in man and the growing knowledge of students and researchers.

Health is your normal and natural state. You were created, designed, and born to be healthy! Let that be your predominant thought and your physical body temple will awaken and respond to experience the healing that is its divine birthright.

Build a Prosperity Consciousness

How would you like to be born the child of J. Paul Getty or a Rockefeller? You would have it made, wouldn't you? So let's follow that line of reasoning. Rich and powerful as some humans are, God is far greater. He is *more* powerful, richer, wiser, more generous. You are born the child of God!

Think about this. If you profess to believe the Bible—and certainly many people on this hemisphere must, for we find it a perennial bestseller and there is hardly a home without a Bible—then you must know that it plainly and explicitly states that God is your Father, that you were born the beloved child of God. Not only that, but it also unequivocally states that you were created in the very image and likeness of God.

You have surely heard friends or relatives say of a baby, "She is the image of her mother!" Look at yourself; no, not the physical garment of flesh you are now wearing, but the living being that uses the garment of flesh. Say to yourself, "I am the image of my Father, God!" Taking the Bible seriously forces you to expand your self-image, doesn't it?

One of the sadly neglected areas of religion is the Bible teachings on prosperity. The Bible teaches that man was born to be rich, and it explains how to claim that birthright, how to be free. The Bible says, "A thousand may fall at your side, ten thousand at your right hand; but it will not come near you"—Psalms 91:7. At one time this was read as though it were merely nice, poetic Bible verse to be memorized and recited to show that one was among the "good guys." Today we are beginning to realize that this is more than ancient sacred poetry. It is the statement of a principle, a principle that is just as valid and practical and provable as any principle in a physics textbook.

The principle is this: when we keep our thinking right—that is, in tune with God, consistent with the spiritual Truth that there is only one Power and one Presence in the universe and that this Power and Presence is only good—then no matter what suggestions of threatening disaster or even discouraging facts surround us, we will not be harmed; *"it will not come near"* us. Hard to believe? It is if we are not used to *believing* the Bible. It is possible to worship the Bible, rather than believe it and apply its teachings.

God is your Father. When Jesus spoke of *your*

Father, He meant the father of each individual; He meant you, the individual who is reading these words right now. God is *your* Father; *your* spiritual Parent! God loves you. Agreed? Maybe you think you are unworthy and that God does not love you. But the Truth is that God loves you completely and forever, beyond any human limitation, for He beholds you as you are in spiritual reality, free from fault: radiant, beautiful, eternal, His own beloved child.

God is the creative First Cause of all that is. In short, He is the origin and source of all the potentialities, the resources, the supply for any possible need; God is the inexhaustible storehouse. You are the beloved child of a Father who is infinitely wealthy, infinitely wise, and infinitely powerful.

What is missing? Why are you eating "husks"? Why are you emotionally upset over economic statistics? So-called experts can predict what they like; but what is going to happen to you as an individual is not dependent on their predictions. Your destiny is dependent on your own emotional states and attitudes!

Life is an individual matter, not a collective one. If many people seem to be in the same boat, it is because each of them is thinking the same negative thoughts and believing the same limited beliefs. Let any individual change his mental beliefs and he immediately "leaves the boat."

100

How do you change your thinking concerning "hard times"? How do you get out of a boat that is shooting the rapids and heading toward—heaven only knows what? You climb up and out, into a prosperity consciousness, by following the basic Bible teachings that are amplified in New Thought. We teach that the kingdom of God is within man. We teach that you were born a child of God, with all the authority and power that go with such a high birth. We teach that it is your Father's good pleasure to give you the kingdom. We reiterate Jesus' words, "Whatever you ask in prayer, believe that you receive it, and you will" —Mark 11:24.

We need to emphasize these positive aspects about who and what we are before we can tap into the inexhaustible riches and prosperity that eternally exist in the kingdom of God. We must overcome some extremely hardened false and limited beliefs about ourselves and about life!

A person who thinks of himself as helpless, insignificant, and "only human" hasn't a chance in the world of breaking through the hardened crust of false and limited beliefs that hold him in poverty, bondage, and perpetual pressure. One such limited belief that many people firmly cling to is that supply means money. "Let's see you get along without money," they argue. "Let's see you buy a car or pay your electric bill without money!" Yes, the concept that supply is money, or something material that you can trade or barter, is the crystallized belief of those who walk in spiritual darkness.

It takes a special kind of courage to break through that long-accepted belief and take hold of the unlimited belief that *supply is consciousness.* Prosperous conditions, including money, are *effects;* mind, thought, and feeling are *causes.* To change an effect or to bring about a desired effect, you must work in the realm of cause—of mind, thought, feeling.

What thought will *cause* the effect of prosperity, abundance, fulfillment of every need? This thought will, *God is the source of my supply!* The secret is not just in repeating the words. Repeating words isn't thought. The words are just signals, symbols, signposts, that point to something deeper—a principle that must be accepted.

Perhaps you can see now why we needed to begin this lesson with a reminder of who and what we really are—a Biblically legitimate child of God, whom God intended to express as we were created: the image and likeness of the Father. Our true nature is unlimited good, if the Bible is to be believed, for in Genesis it is stated "And God saw everything that he had made, and behold, it was very good"—Genesis 1:31.

We need to hold to this Truth because it is very difficult, from the level of thinking of ourself as helpless, insignificant, only-human beings, to begin to "get into" and totally believe the principle behind the words, *God is the source of my supply.* The only-human person thinks of God as a King on a throne in outer space and of himself as just one of hundreds of millions of human-ants scurrying around on this tiny, whirling globe. He thinks, How will God get the supply to me? I see no possible way except through a miracle, and miracles just don't happen to me. So he runs around in his little self-imposed prison of limited beliefs, believing that the world of facts and appearances is permanent or changeable only through the sweat of his brow or the cunning of his intellect.

With a right thought about yourself, one based on the word of Jesus—that you are not "only human"—you can burst through the self-imposed prison of limited beliefs. Like so many things, it is the thinking about doing it that scares you and holds you back.

What was the hardest thing about your first dive off a high board, or taking your first drivers' test? Wasn't it just thinking about it? Wouldn't these have been easier if you had thought instead about how long you had practiced and how well you did with your instructor? In short, if you had had confidence in yourself instead of feeling inadequate and afraid everything would have been simpler. In the same way, it is easy to accept totally the belief that God is the source of your supply when you confidently know that you are a spiritual being, a lawful child of God, created in your divine Father's image and likeness.

Once you have the courage to burst loose from the programmed only-human limitation, you begin to live from the inside out, instead of from the outside in. Now you can seriously and sincerely work with the universal principle of cause and effect.

You understand that your environment is a looking glass. What you see there is the projection, the end effect, the result of invisible yet dynamic patterns of thought and feeling. Can you change those mental patterns? You certainly can! One of the first mental patterns you want to work on to change is the belief that outer conditions have power of themselves! You don't have to fight the world. All you have to "fight" is your own fear of the world. The best way of overcoming fear of something or someone is to remind yourself that your God is tremendously stronger than whoever or whatever is trying to frighten you.

You are a child of God, created in His image, having access to all that God is. Is that appearance of poverty or lack, that seeming obstacle to the fulfillment of your need more powerful than the spiritual forces that are your birthright? Let's take the spiritual offensive. Ignore the present conditions that are worrying you and making you a nervous "wreck." Don't deny they exist; ignore them by refusing to dwell on them. Instead, dwell

104

on the principle that God is the source of your supply. Then start directing your faculties of mind from a spiritual basis. For instance, redirect your faculty of imagination. See and feel yourself as experiencing that which you need or long for. The imagination has been called the scissors of the mind, for with it you mentally "cut the pattern" of future form and events.

Imagination is mostly "feeling" rather than "seeing." If you would imagine yourself on a small platform one hundred feet above the ground, the details of the scene would be indistinct, but you could certainly feel the moisture in your palms and the breathless anxiety of actually being in such a spot. Use this imaging faculty for good. Don't emphasize the details—they may yet be indistinct. Dwell instead on how you *feel* experiencing the good.

Also, there is a right use of your mental faculty of *faith*. Faith is the very substance, the raw material, the molten form of things hoped for, the incontrovertible evidence of things not seen. Faith's mountain-moving, miracle-working power turns the most threatening appearance into a mere pussycat!

Magnify your faith-faculty through belief in the Bible teachings about prosperity. The way to prosperity is not to ask God to direct you into ways to get more money, or more power over others so that they do your will, or toward the most profitable investments; that would be "using" God as a sort of chief counselor to you, the boss. You would be trying to fit God into your outer-oriented standards. Prayer would then become a kind of "rabbit's foot," and of course, *sometimes* a rabbit's foot *seems* to work. But there is a better, surer way, a Truth-based way.

The Truth-based way is the Bible teaching of prosperity which hinges on an entire change of mental direction. We need to change from looking to and depending on outer conditions to looking to and depending on the limitless wealth awaiting our discovery in inner space.

If you are experiencing a condition of lack of any kind, here is how to follow through on changing that condition. First, take time to consider the principle that conditions are effects; mind, with its dynamic content of thoughts, attitudes, emotional states, and beliefs, is *cause.* You could experiment mentally with the principle: On Monday, think negative thoughts; find every occasion to get emotional, angry, resentful, hostile, and so forth. Talk about how bad things are; look for pains and symptoms in your body and tell everyone about them. Watch how the day goes. Then on Tuesday be just as fair to the other side of the experiment. Think positive, constructive thoughts. Refuse to react emotionally no matter what the provocation. Look for the good around you and talk about it. Bless your body and take notice of all the organs and muscles that are doing their intricate job so well. See how that day goes! Hopefully, you won't have to do Monday's experiment to prove to yourself that Mind is cause, conditions are effects.

Now, about that condition of lack. Its cause is a mental condition in you, so place your attention there. Work at overcoming any feeling or thought of discouragement or helplessness. How do you do that? By letting a little psychological state called "hope" get its foot in your mental door. Hope might be translated as a feeling that you will try.

Try changing your mental outlook. Try not to dwell on how bad things may presently look. Try not to take the tempting mental dead-end path called, "If only . . ." "If only someone would leave me some money; if only I had a better education; if only . . ." Well, you know how you can occupy yourself endlessly on the "if only" merry-go-round.

Here's an example of how to get off that merry-go-round. Let's say you own a business and things aren't going so well at present. One thing after the other seems to prevent your success. Change your mental attitude by thinking in terms of protecting your business from adverse conditions by right thought. You take out insurance to protect your business; why not take out some "success insurance"? The premiums don't cost you a cent; all you have to do is think in terms of success and keep doubt out of your mind. Think of God as the real Owner of your business. It is His responsibility. You are working for and with Him. Can God fail?

If you are an employee, don't stew and fret about someone getting more money or a better position than you, or about the fear of being laid-off. Instead, feel that you are working for God. Your raise, or your promotion, or your job itself doesn't come from your employer; it comes from your consciousness, and *through* your employer. The greediest, tightest employer in the world cannot stand against the power of the consciousness of a child of God. He will either give, or he will be taken out of the way; that is, you will be effortlessly led to a channel of supply that fits your expanded consciousness.

If you are presently unemployed, say to yourself: *In the great universal scheme, there is a place especially created for me. This universe is whole and I am a part of its wholeness.* A thought like this will draw you to your right place like a magnet! Then, take action; follow every lead even though you feel sure it is of no use; for in the action of taking a lead, infinite wisdom may be setting up the divine order and timing for the right place to open up for you and through you.

Remember this; *God is the source of your supply!* All else are channels—jobs, inheritances, stocks, refunds, customers—all channels. You tap into the Source of your supply by realizing that outer conditions do not have the ultimate say-so over your life and circumstances, unless you let them by believing that they do!

The Truth is that you as an individual have control over your life and circumstances through your choice of thoughts, beliefs, attitudes, and emotional responses. There have been, there are now, and there always will be hard times for those who look exclusively to the outer world of facts. Good times for you as an individual, as a child of God, are "at hand"—even within you—when you come to yourself and base your thoughts and beliefs on the simple Truth that the Bible teaches: God is the source of your supply, and henceforth you can depend on God, instead of people, conditions, and outer circumstances. Prosper by believing. Place your faith in the power of God.

Win Without Effort

Are you tired of living a limited life—a life that often seems lusterless, dull, filled with one problem after another? Are you tired of feeling like a loser instead of a winner? You can change all that. Your life can be changed in any direction you want it changed, whenever you want to change it.

Once a friend said to me: "I'm sick of it all. There seems to be no meaning or purpose to life. I didn't ask to be born, but here I am. All my life there has always been something to worry about, and it never stops. Life," he went on, "is like being pushed into deep water when you don't know how to swim. You don't want to drown and you don't know how to swim, so you just keep thrashing around desperately trying to stay afloat. What's the purpose of it all?"

Obviously, my friend was in a pretty dark mood. When we are going through a challenge like this, it is often good to express our feelings to someone else. We may find that the answer to our problems lies in our very questions. For instance, remember that my friend said, "Life is like being pushed into deep water when you don't know how to swim." There is his answer—*learn to swim!* To me, the greatest textbook for learning how to swim in the deep waters of life is the Bible, particularly the teachings of Jesus.

The first lesson in learning how to swim in the sea of life, how to master the swift currents and avoid the rocks and whirlpools, is the same lesson that comes first in meeting a healing or prosperity challenge. It is to learn *who* you really are. The Bible tells us in the first few pages a great secret about our real ancestry. It says, "So God created man in his own image, in the image of God he created him"—Genesis 1:27.

The word *man* as used here is naturally used in its generic sense. That is, it means all men and women; it means the species homo sapiens. You are a member of that species. You were created in the image of God.

Now let's follow the analogy of the swimmer. If we were learning to swim, the instructor would first have a little talk with us, perhaps saying something like this: "Look, the first thing you need to understand is that you are *potentially* able to become an *expert* swimmer. You may not be able to swim now, but this doesn't mean you can't learn. You will not only learn how to tread water, but also you will become so skillful at swimming dangerous waters that you will actually get a supreme pleasure out of meeting and conquering the seeming obstacles and threats!"

And isn't this what the Bible is saying also? The Bible says, in effect: My child, in these opening pages I want to impress upon you the Truth that you have infinite potentiality. You are wondrously made. You are created after the image and likeness of the universal life Principle that created all things. You are created after the image and likeness of God!

Now we return to our swimming instructor to listen in on the next words used to teach a beginner how to master the sport. He would probably continue by saying: "Now there are certain laws of flotation, laws of physics, that will be working for you if you work with them and not against them.

"For instance, if you hold air in your lungs and lie on the water very still, there is a law of physics that enables you to float on the water; and this will rest you when you feel tired. There are other laws of physics working for you. For instance, when you push water away from you with your cupped hands, this action propels you forward."

The Bible tells us there are spiritual laws that are universal. This means that they are always available, always in activity, and that they always work for anyone who applies them.

There is the law of mind action. The nature of

our thoughts determines the nature of the conditions in the environment of our life. As we "think in our hearts," so are we. There is what we might call the law of spiritual floating when we want to rest and renew our energy. The Bible says it this way: "Thou dost keep him in perfect peace, whose mind is stayed on thee, because he trusts in thee"—Isaiah 26:3. In other words, let go and let God. Get still and know that underneath are the everlasting arms, forever holding us up.

This is the "immediate action" step that you can take when you are in trouble. It is short, simple, and effective. Simply *Let go and let God!*

This is not just a comforting thought; nor is it a religious escape hatch to avoid facing up to our problems and responsibilities. It is a spiritually scientific principle for meeting life successfully. The principle behind the words let go and let God is that universal creative energy flows to and through you more effectively when your mind is "loose," when you are calm and quiet inwardly. Think how often a swimmer is saved from drowning by simply relaxing, ceasing to struggle, and floating effortlessly for a time. The same principle often applies in life's "waters."

This is not just opinion; it is spiritual Law. "Spiritual law," the skeptic replies. "What makes you think it is spiritual law?" In our New Thought approach to the Bible, we think of the Scriptures as a textbook, a "law book" of right living.

We have a great deal of knowledge about how to do many things. We can go to schools to learn how to build a radio, or a bridge, or a space capsule, and nearly anything else. We learn how to read and write, add and subtract. There are training programs to show us how to do almost anything, except how to live happily, productively, successfully!

Just to learn the principles for this essential "how to" from the Bible is not enough; we must use them, apply them. We must get into the water and give our lessons a real try. But the trouble is, just when we most need what we have learned, we often disregard it. It is so easy to see where others need to apply Truth principles. We may think, for instance, If only Uncle George would stop struggling and just let go and let God, surely he could get out of his difficulties. Then we are suddenly faced with some threatening challenge to our own well-being—deep waters in our own experience—and we go to pieces and start thrashing about, forgetting our Truth principles. Much of the Truth we have learned and agreed with in the pleasant moments of living seems to dissolve when we are called upon to apply it.

Several years ago a friend of mine who owned a small business was doing fairly well, with only a small amount of worries that go with a business. Then one day it happened. The building from which he leased space for his store was sold, and he was given a comparatively short time to vacate the premises.

He was a Truth student, but he immediately began to struggle. "The unfairness!" he raved. "Twenty years of building a clientele at this location, and now I have to start all over. I'm not as young as I used to be." On and on his thoughts whirlpooled. But as you can see, it is at just such a time that we need God. Times like these are when so many of us shut God out by trying to or thinking that they must take the whole job.

But God works in mysterious and wonderful ways. Although we may forget God—forget the universal spiritual law—the eternal, all-wise, all-loving Power never forgets us and never ceases to be active according to divine principle. God often works in ways that at the time seem inconsistent with our good; but in the long run, we see that He is always working for our highest good.

My friend, the evicted businessman, came down with a serious physical challenge. Surely doctors would say that there was a definite connection between his illness and his negative mental and emotional reaction to business problems. While lying flat on his back in the hospital, he came to the realizations that there was nothing he could do about the store situation and that getting well was the most important thing. He let go of the problem. Today my friend has a larger store, in a newer building, in a better location. He has a larger clientele than ever, and it is still growing. He is happier and more successful because through the apparent catastrophe of the eviction, plus the additional "hurricane" of the illness, he learned a great lesson. He learned that he is not alone; that when he runs into something that seems more powerful than his human ability to handle, he can release the problem, "float" spiritually, and let the all-capable Force of the spiritual universe take over.

Let's not wait for a hurricane to teach us that although we have human limitations, we also have access to divine potential. When we seem to be at the end of our human limit of strength, we have only to switch over to the infinite power of our spiritual Resource.

To "let go and let God" does not mean that you are getting yourself out of the picture. Rather, it means that you are remembering to let God into the picture. When trouble suddenly and unexpectedly stirs up in your life, it is only natural to stagger a bit, to lose your spiritual equilibrium. And while you are in this vulnerable position, you may gulp down a host of fears which come rushing in and flood your consciousness. The first thing you know, you feel tense and choked up with negative thoughts and feelings. It is then that you need to say to yourself: "Whoa! Relax. Let go and let God."

Perhaps you will have to say this several times,

but soon you will feel a settling down within you, a kind of calm arising. This will be followed by a feeling of confidence as you remember that all of the beneficent forces of the universe are rallying to your aid, bearing you up, sustaining you.

Many people have asked if letting go means not doing anything about the problem. No, it doesn't. What you are letting go of are certain negative and strangling states of mind. Remember that there is a distinction between you and the states of mind that may be in your consciousness at any given time. When you say or think, "I am afraid," what you really mean is that the unchanging "I" or "I am" of you is attached to or aware of a mental state or feeling of fear that has entered your field of consciousness. You are temporarily trying to hold onto a rock to keep from drowning, when instead you need only accept the life-preserver of freeing Truth.

You see, you have absolute control over the contents of your consciousness. When you say, "I let go and let God," you are ordering mental states of fear and strangling anxiety to go, and welcoming into your field of consciousness a mental state of faith in God. You cease to struggle with the weight of the problem; you release it and let the Truth of your being buoy you up.

Even if the explanation sounds complex, the application is simple and the results measurable. The next time you feel uptight over anything—

from making a difficult telephone call to coping with a seemingly gloomy medical diagnosis—apply spiritual immediate action, and affirm with ease and conviction, *I now let go and let God!* Thereby you open yourself to the harmonious, healing, miracle-working power of the kingdom of God within you.

Now is a good time to begin to apply this principle to make a fresh start in your inner life. Relax, release, and let go. Let go of past mistakes. Let go of past heartaches. Let go of past failures. Let go of those times when you did not meet the high standards you set for yourself. Let go of memory-barnacles that are slowing down the ship of your life. Let the universal principle of Truth carry you to the goal for which you have set your course. Let God do His perfect work.

With these ideas in mind, we can return again to our swimming instructor. After reassuring the one who desires to learn how to swim that he has the basic innate ability to become an expert swimmer, and after telling him of some of the laws involved in swimming and how to work with them then he may say, "Okay, now jump into the water and let's practice the kicking-your-feet principle."

If the student doesn't get into the water, he will never learn to swim. Or if he gets into the water and doesn't practice as best he can, he will never learn to swim. So it is with learning to live successfully and abundantly. We have to cease giving excuses and start trusting this invisible and intangible power we call God. Sure it is difficult. It is difficult for the one learning to swim to launch out and trust these laws that he has been told about. That *water* around him seems threatening he may think: What if the laws shouldn't work this time? What if I can't work them correctly? Oh no, I'd sink! That would be the end of me.

We too may look at the difficult problem that faces us and think, Religion is all right in church, where everybody is dressed up and looking reverent. The stained glass windows, the choir, the clergyman at the pulpit, all make it easy to believe in God. But I'm alone now in this personal storm—here in my office, at home, out there on the highway. How do I *know* things will work out in a right and perfect way if I let go and trust this unseen and unfelt Power?

The person who eventually becomes a good swimmer is the one who overcomes his fears and doubts and takes a chance, if you want to put it that way. Are you willing to take a chance on God? You who may be facing some difficult problem, you who may be worried about a son or daughter, you who may have a financial problem that could ruin you, you who feel discouraged and beaten— are you willing to take a chance on God?

It takes courage, but if you are willing, a whole new life will open up to you! No, I'm not going to say foolishly that a miracle will happen to change you overnight or that the problem will be entirely solved instantaneously. This certainly can happen and might happen, but it would be foolish to guarantee that it would. But there is a guarantee: *something* will happen! Some new avenue of action will open, some break in the problem will occur that will give you new encouragement and hope.

Most of all, you will develop a new attitude about life even though you realize that there are still problem areas to be met. You will have that wonderfully exhilarating feeling that you now know the secret of how to meet them. This is akin to that feeling of the one learning to swim when, after striking out on his own—even though he might be awkward and he might flail the water clumsily at first—something happens within him. He suddenly knows that the instructor was right, that with practice he *can* overcome the threat, that he *can* master the water, and best of all, he no longer fears the water, but finds it a friend, a servant, a blessing!

Here is a way to start: Picture a group of people in a swimming class, and imagine that you are among them. The instructor says, "Everyone has the potential ability to swim gracefully. You have the physical equipment, and if you follow my instructions, you will be complying with the laws of physics that will carry you through the water gracefully." Then think to yourself, *Jesus, my spiritual Teacher, is telling me that I can master life. He says that I have the equipment, which is my mind, my ability to think and choose my thoughts. And He says that if I follow His instructions, I will be complying with universal, undeviating spiritual law that will work to restore order, harmony, health, prosperity, happiness, and peace in my life.*

He said, "Whatever you ask in prayer, believe that you receive it, and you will"—Mark 11:24. All right, what is your problem? Say to yourself, "I wholeheartedly follow the instructions of my Teacher, Jesus. I *believe* that I am receiving the answer to my problem. I believe that all things are working out in an amazingly wonderful and perfect way. I am grateful!"

Then go about your day's work, determined to hold the attitude that the right and perfect answer is now manifesting. It is just a matter of time, and you are leaving the timing up to God's all-knowing wisdom. Don't be afraid, don't doubt—jump into the water and swim! Be buoyed up by spiritual principles and you will find you are on your way to mastering life's problems. You are a born winner when you work with God and His never-failing spiritual law.

Move a Mountain

Have you ever said, "If only I had more faith"? Let's analyze this thing called faith and discuss ways to increase our divine faculty of faith in God.

Faith is a power accessible to everyone and free for the taking. It will enable anyone to overcome every challenge, every seeming handicap or obstacle that confronts, no matter how insurmountable it may seem. Anyone can get more of this power. There is no cost, there are no special requirements, except these: determination and perseverance.

Remember the pictures of a scrawny weakling in Charles Atlas ads years ago? He was always being pushed around by a bully in front of his girl-friend. Then the weakling would send in for the Charles Atlas body-building course, and the next picture would show him with bulging muscles, admired by all the girls on the beach, with all the bullies keeping their distance from him. A good deal of persevering practice and unflagging

122

desire are implied between the comparison of the first picture to the second. Why do we often think that the development of faith is any different than this? We know that anything valuable, any talent or skill takes time, practice, and deep-rooted desire. But somehow we think spiritual know-how and power should just be given to us without any requirements because we have been "big" enough, good-hearted enough, condescending enough to ask God for them.

Although God offers His limitless power and all-knowing wisdom freely, it is we who need to learn how to accept them. You may ask: "What do you mean? What's to learn about accepting?" Here is an example of what I mean: vizualize a subject who has been told by a hypnotist that the room is freezing cold. The room is actually a comfortable seventy-two degrees. If you were to approach the hypnotized subject and try to get him to accept the fact that the room is not freezing, but comfortable, you couldn't do it. He would stand there shivering and being uncomfortable, unable to accept the fact that the room is warm. Anyone acquainted with hypnotism will assure you that the subject will not accept your loving help if contrary to the suggestion. He will continue to shiver under the hypnotist's suggestion that the room is freezing.

It is this same principle that makes it so difficult for us to accept God's help. It is a well-known fact that the mind is extremely suggestible. The basis of hypnotic demonstrations is the suggestibility of the human mind. There are, of course, degrees of suggestibility. That is why in a public demonstration many persons will be offered a simple suggestion but only those who respond the most quickly and completely will be asked to participate.

The suggestibility of the mind is what makes it so difficult for us to accept God's help. We have been concentrating on the outer facts of our problem, fixing our attention on the impossibility of it working out. We have been focusing our thoughts on negative consequences that could logically result from outer facts. We have accepted the "suggestion" of outer appearances so completely that we are hypnotized by them. We mistakenly accept the belief that circumstances are indeed impossible to change and therefore negative consequences are inevitable.

Just as the shivering subject in hypnosis is obviously and painfully uncomfortable even though relief through a change of thought is at hand, so do we suffer, cry, and cringe in the face of our problem, when the Truth is at hand—only a change of thought, a change of belief away!

A snap of the hypnotist's fingers shakes the subject loose from the "spell" of the suggestion. But shaking ourself loose from the spell of outer appearances is not quite that easy. All of our life we have centered our attention outward. We have been programmed to believe that "facts are facts," and that the only way to change them is to introduce more powerful facts into the outer situation.

Faith, to use a definition given in the Bible, is the "assurance of things hoped for, the conviction of things not seen"—Heb. 11:1. To the outer-oriented, appearance-fixed mind, this is a contradiction of terms. Try to get unseen evidence introduced at a trial, or try to prove something with unseen evidence. Everyone knows that the very word *evidence* means something you can see and touch. So when our conscious mind says, in effect, *I want to have faith in the unseen presence of God,* the power of a lifetime of belief in the reality, supremacy, and finality of outer facts comes forth from the subconscious to interfere. We find ourself inwardly shaking with fear, even as we voice the words desiring faith.

Is there an anwer? Certainly there is. We can get more faith in God; it is free, no cost, no special requirements except for *determination* and *perseverance.* The first thing we have to do is to get a toehold in the subconscious mind, to wedge into that massive, hardened, crystallized belief that facts are facts and can only be changed by more powerful facts.

The way to get a wedge under this "mountain," is by using a mental tool called an *affirmation.* An

125

affirmation is a statement of Truth; not a statement of the outer facts. It is a statement of the Truth within the situation. The following would be a good example of a statement of Truth about a factually threatening outer circumstance: *I refuse to be intimidated by the way things appear. I tenaciously cling to an inner conviction that the invisible presence and power of God are working for my good and for the highest good of all concerned in this factual situation. I am grateful!*

This is a start; but it is only a start. We need determination and perseverance! Be persistent. Stick with it. Keep repeating affirmations in times of meditation and prayer. Think about them while doing the many things that require only little conscious attention—such as brushing teeth, shaving, walking to the mailbox. Ordinarily we might waste those moments by worrying or being mentally lazy. We have lots of free time to worry and go over and over problem conditions, lots of free time to convince ourself that things are terrible, devastating, hopeless. We have lots of time to visualize how the situation can hurt us. We have lots of time to make affirmations too.

To think about God's presence, to think about the nonvisible Truth of the situation much of the time may at first seem impossible; but it is not. We can *try.* Every time we try, that wedge goes deeper into the only thing that holds back our perfect answer—the mountain of limited belief that facts and conditions have more power than God's universal and indwelling Spirit.

When we work at cultivating this deep-rooted faith in God, we build a lasting treasure or resource. It is ours for all time. Whatever mountainous problem may confront us at this or another time, we can be sure our faith will help us meet it. As we work at programming ourself to have faith in the invisible spiritual reality of life, taking it to the dynamic depths of our being to meet the present challenge, we will find that the next challenge (and there is sure to be another) will be easier to handle. In fact, this is the way to measure our spiritual progress. It is not uncommon for Truth students to say, "No matter how long I study and practice Truth, I always feel that there is so much more to learn. I wonder if I'm making any progress at all!" That's the characteristic of Truth—one can never encompass all of it. We can't wrap it up in a package or book and say, "that's it." It is an ever-unfolding process. We will always feel a little "green" at it. But remember, when we're "green," we're growing!

One way to measure progress is by taking time to notice that certain situations or problems that would have knocked us for a loop, devastated us with anxiety a year ago, can now be handled easily without getting unstrung or upset.

Faith is a faculty of mind that is an integral part of each of us. Heretofore we have focused that faculty of faith in only one direction—outward. We have had faith in certain people, faith that the sun would come up tomorrow, faith in the pilot of the plane we ride in, faith in the reliability of the news report of a story. That's all right; there is nothing inherently wrong with having faith in things and people. But our faculty of faith was designed to encompass more than just what you can see and touch, what our five senses can report to you. It is designed also to focus *inward* and see or be aware of the invisible presence of God, with just as much assurance of God's reality as we have of the realness of the visible world. As we learn to develop this inward aspect of faith, we come to understand that, whereas the outer things we have faith in are changeable and unpredictable, the invisible spiritual principles are unchanging, powerful, and more to be relied upon.

Jesus claimed some amazing things for faith, didn't He? He said it would move a mountain. This may sound like a big order; perhaps He didn't literally mean it—or perhaps He did! We can agree that Jesus intended us to know that faith is a fantastic power. No matter how mountainlike a problem may appear to us, faith can move it out of our way.

Jesus taught that faith is the miracle healer. He didn't say, "*I* have healed you." He said, "Your faith has made you well"—Matthew 9:22. Jesus claimed for faith the power to prosper you and to

128

fulfill your every need, from the smallest to the largest. "Whatever you ask in prayer, believe that you receive it, and you will"—Mark 11:24.

It is about time that we investigated more deeply this all-accomplishing power that Jesus talked so much about. It is time that we took the Bible seriously, instead of treating it as a sort of sacred ornament in the home. The Bible claims there is a power that will move mountains, yet we continue to try to move the mountains in our life with our fingernails. Actually, there is a reason why we don't take advantage of this tremendous and free-for-the-asking power. The reason is that we do not know *how* to use it, develop it, focalize it. We don't know enough about the principle behind the operation of the power of faith. Any kind of power is useless in the hands of someone who doesn't know how to use it.

This brings us to the first point about faith: it *is* a power. Although it is true that power is useless in the hands of someone who doesn't know how to use it, it is also true that power is dangerous in the hands of someone who doesn't know the principle of its right use!

The power of faith can be dangerous because the formative power of wrongly directed faith becomes *fear!* Does that surprise you? Fear is really wrongly-directed faith. What is fear, but faith that things are going to turn out in an unfavorable way? Job discovered too late the formative power

129

of fear when he exclaimed, "For the thing that I fear comes upon me, and what I dread befalls me"—Job 3:25.

Job was talking about the same formative power that Jesus spoke of, "According to your faith, be it done unto you." Jesus is referring to faith rightly-directed. Job is revealing the results of faith wrongly-directed.

This is the first important point to remember: fear and faith have the same emotive power. What makes the difference is the nature of the thoughts in our mind through which this formative power passes. If our thoughts are predominantly negative, they are thoughts which, if verbalized, may say: "I am a failure. Nothing good ever happens to me. This deal will probably fall through," or "Our marriage is on the rocks. I am doomed to a life of unhappiness. Nothing could ever change the way things are," or "The doctor seemed awfully concerned to put me in the hospital right away. I am afraid to imagine what terrible trouble lies in store for me."

No one can be blamed for having these negative thoughts. Much of our negative thinking can be rationalized as being "realistic." Perhaps we *have* lost out on many opportunities. Perhaps the marriage is at an emotional *impasse*. Perhaps the hospital experience does look frightening. The point is that, although no one can be blamed for entertaining such negative thoughts, no one has to harbor them in his mental household. We do not have to invite negativity to occupy the guest room of our consciousness for an indefinite stay. This is especially true, now that we know that negative thoughts will short-circuit the constructive power of faith and bring upon us just what we have feared.

What we all need to do more of is to live in the present moment and keep our mental fingers out of the future. Sometimes I think we are too intellectual for our own good. We reason, Things have been like this for a long time, getting worse all the time; therefore unless something miraculous happens (which I can't imagine possible), things will continue to get worse.

That might make good intellectual reasoning, but it certainly doesn't make good spiritual reasoning! In the first place, with our knowledge of the spiritual law of mind action, we realize that thoughts or beliefs that we totally accept have to outpicture themselves in our world. So we know that our intellectual reasoning, by its very often negative nature, can doom us to a repetition of the failure-filled past.

In the second place, with our knowledge of the almightiness of God, the immediacy of God's presence, the willingness of God to help us, there is every reason to believe that what we call "something miraculous" can and will enter the picture to *change* our old course.

It all comes down to the one simple proposition; either we do or do not really believe in and totally accept the belief that there is a transcendent, creative, life-giving, loving, success-producing Power that we call God. If we believe in an invisible, infinitely intelligent, all-powerful, all-loving Presence and Principle which works through divine law, then we will never agree to the seemingly logical, but false thinking. We will never agree that because appearances look unchangeable and have been unchanged in the past, the future necessarily holds more of the same. God is not limited by precedent. The fact that a thing has never been done before is not proof that it cannot be done. There is a difference between "never having been done before" and being "impossible."

"Expect a miracle!" It breaks up mountains of crystallized fear thoughts. It reminds me of little David going up to Goliath, armed with only a slingshot. How do we picture David? Do we see him as being afraid—shaking all over, cringing? No—we see him calm and confident. He had confidence in his ability to handle a slingshot, and he had confidence in God's invisible power and presence helping him.

The phrase *expect a miracle* is our David. Let the multitude of our thought-people cry out and be dismayed at how our Goliath-problem is so huge and invincible. But then, let us say to ourself, "I expect a miracle." As our heart hears those words, the cries of the multitude of our negative thought-people subside and become quiet. David has stepped forth. The Goliath-problem may still be standing there leering at us, but because we are applying the Truth of the Bible, we know the ending; Goliath cannot stand.

The logic behind the words, *expect a miracle* is indisputable if one admits to even the slightest belief in God. Of course, if we have a papier-mâche god—if God is just a word that we pretend to believe in—then the word *miracle* is empty and meaningless to us. If we can accept the belief that the Bible is right—that there is God's creative power and principle that transcends us and yet is capable of moving in and through us to establish order and harmony, to bring forth perfect solutions—then the word *miracle* becomes a very acceptable and appropriate word to explain what happens when God's power is released into a problem that appears difficult from a human point of view.

The divine power is released through what we might call faith-thinking. There is faith-thinking and there is fear-thinking. One shuttles the formative power toward shaping desirable conditions (faith-thinking); the other shuttles the formative power toward shaping unhappy conditions (fear-thinking). It is as simple as that.

Check up on your thoughts. They will tell your

fortune. They will unveil your future. But here is the freeing Truth: at any time, in any situation, you can change from fear-thinking to faith-thinking. You can move a mountain!

What is it that is on your mind today? No matter whether it is a seemingly small matter or a really dire problem, change from fear-thinking to faith-thinking. Say to yourself right now: "I am not going to make matters worse—I am not going to add to the mountain—by entertaining any negative thoughts about the future outcome of this situation, no matter how dark or threatening things presently look. When I think about it, I am going to take the position that things are going to work out in a right and perfect way. Nothing is wrong with expecting a miracle, because my positive, faith-thinking does release the transcendent power of God into a human situation."

Picture a freshly-plowed field. There is a power in that field that will grow whatever seeds are dropped into it. You can sow weed seeds or you can sow useful seeds. The ground doesn't care; it will give you back whatever you sow. The field is your mind. The power that grows seeds in the field is the universal creative Principle. The seeds are your thoughts. Faith-thinking is sowing faith; and the harvest next week, or next month, or next summer will be like unto the faith-seeds you are sowing today.

Don't be concerned about the fear-weeds you may have sown in the past. If you will let the faith-seeds predominate now (because they are strong and healthy and partake of God's nature) they will grow into abundant fulfillment and leave no space for the weeds to grow. Remember the teachings of the Master, "If you have faith as a grain of mustard seed, you will say to this mountain, 'Move hence to yonder place,' and it will move; and nothing will be impossible to you"—Matthew 17:20.

Expand Your Vision

Are you content with the way things are in your life, or do you feel that you should be more, do more, have more? Would you like to increase your enjoyment of life and your effectiveness in solving problems? Perhaps these are really unfair questions, because from what I have learned and experienced through the years, almost everyone feels that he has not yet reached his full potential; that given the chance, he could do, be, and have much more than at present. So, if your answer to these questions is yes, this lesson is for you.

The desire to expand is not really vanity, nor is it wishful thinking; it is but the irrepressible urging of the divine in us. What are we to do about this subtle uneasiness, our divine discontent with things as they are? Let's meet this challenge with a two-phase positive approach.

PHASE 1 - YOUR MENTAL REAR-VISION MIRROR

The first phase of our lesson is to bring our energy out of the area of the dead past and into the focus of the eternal *now*. Too many of us waste too much time, emotional energy, and nervous energy in looking backward, in going over the past. By breaking or at least controlling this negative habit of dwelling on the past, we can release tremendous amounts of energy for successfully solving problems at hand.

I have many occasions to counsel—perhaps I should really say "talk"—with people about their problems. The word *counsel* seems to imply the giving of advice. And, of course, the only counsel or advice I can give is whatever a person already knows before he comes to me. That is, we all have access to unlimited wisdom and strength and guidance within us. I do not know the answers to the infinite number of problems that human beings face today; but I *do* know where to find the answers. The answers lie in the one Mind in which each of us is a center of consciousness; or to use the simple language of Jesus, the answer is found in the Father within.

I can't go into the Father-Mind for *your* answer, nor can you go within to find answers for me. Even as each problem is personal to you and brought about by you—by your actions, thoughts, attitudes, and your response to events and people in your life—so is each *answer* personal to you. Your answer can come forth only through you— through your actions, thoughts, and attitudes.

In talking with many people about their problems, I have found that almost ninety percent of their thoughts and conversations seem to deal with the past. They go over and over the details and events that led up to their present state of despair. They repeat word for word conversations they had with parties involved a month ago, sometimes even a year or more ago. Many times they zero in on one event or decision of the past that they feel was the turning point, the start of all their trouble. They seem to almost get a masochistic enjoyment out of "kicking" themselves over and over for the one wrong decision or event.

In the first phase of expanding the vision toward a positive direction, we need to stop looking backward and dwelling on how we came to this point. If we don't, we are only racing our engines and spinning our wheels, getting nowhere. The thing to do is to tell ourself that the past is gone. There is nothing we can do about it. The only thing we have to work with is the present, and the way we handle this moment will determine the direction our future will take.

Every car has a rear-vision mirror, a very handy and necessary piece of equipment. But what would happen if one drove down the street looking only or mostly in the rear-vision mirror? Our memory is a sort of rear-vision mirror. It will show us, in the present moment, where we have been, what we have gone past, and what we have gone through. This can serve a good and important purpose many times. We can see where we have made a mistake, and that is good. Once we have seen it, we can release it and place our vision back on the road in front of us.

Another way of constructively using our memory is to glance back at times when we have been extremely successful at something. We can go even as far back as when, perhaps, we won that trip selling the most new subscriptions on our paper route. We worked hard and persistently for that reward, didn't we? We lay awake nights thinking of new approaches or new people to see. Then that wonderful day came when it was announced in front of all our peers that *we* had won. Wasn't that a great feeling? Feel it again for a while.

That's enough—let's get our eyes back on the road ahead now. We will still feel the thrill and the confidence of that victory of many years ago, and it will help us to negotiate the present difficult road ahead with more faith and confidence.

This is the interesting thing about the memory; it is a function of the subconscious mind. All these pictures and feelings are stored in the silent walls of our subconscious level of mind. Now here is a peculiar thing about the subconscious: when we call for a picture from the past and it is shown on the screen of our conscious mind, our subconscious is not able to judge whether it is really happening, or whether we are just viewing a picture of what happened in the past. As far as the subconscious mind is concerned, it is happening *now.*

For instance, think of that time in the past when you were on a high ladder painting the house. You looked down and felt all funny inside; your palms began to perspire. As you vividly recall that scene, you may find your palms beginning to perspire *now.* Why? Because your subconscious is reacting as if it were actually happening *now.*

Knowing this, we can see how self-defeating it is to relive an unhappy, embarrassing, or frightening experience. We will deplete our emotional, nervous, and physical energy, just as if it were actually happening again.

By eliminating or at least controlling the habit of dwelling on the past, we will have more actual strength—emotional and physical—to handle present problems. Jesus taught the lesson we are discussing by using the analogy of a farmer and a plow. He said, "No one who puts his hand to the plow and looks back is fit for the kingdom of God"—Luke 9:62. Obviously, this is an illustration; if it were taken literally, it would have no practical meaning except to one who plows the ground. But when we seek the principle that

Jesus is getting at through this analogy, we can find some good, solid advice on solving our problems more effectively.

The "field' of this analogy is our life—the minutes, hours, and days of our life—the events and circumstances of our life. The "plow" is our mind or our thinking, for it is by means of our mind and thinking that we prepare the soil or conditions of our life.

The idea of "looking back" represents centering our attention on the past—looking where we have been and at what we have done wrong. And in steering a plow, this is just as disastrous as driving a car by looking in the rear-vision mirror.

As we visualize the picture that Jesus evokes in our mind through this illustration, we can see what is happening. The plowman is looking back while the plow is moving forward. The obvious result is that the plow is making a crooked furrow. And, in continuing to look back, the plowman may curse in his frustration about the crooked furrows in his field, but as long as he continues this way, the furrows don't get any better. Likewise, as long as we keep looking back at the past, life never will get any better.

The story further illustrates what Jesus taught over and over in so many other illustrations—that the kingdom of God is not a place in a geographical or physical sense. The kingdom of God is a place in consciousness, it is a state of consciousness we can only enter when our attention is in the present moment. Therefore, if our mind is clogged with unhappy memories of the past, if we are mentally busy hashing over what is done, we are not "fit" for the kingdom of God. "Fit," according to a dictionary, means, "able, suitable, qualified." If we are dwelling on the past, we certainly are not *able* to enter the kingdom of God whose only entrance is in the *now!*

How does all this relate to our present problem or challenge? First, we resolve that we will stop going over the conversations, feelings, and events of the past. We will stop trying to justify our past actions. Start from scratch, start with a clean page. Here is the problem the way it is *now*. What should we do about it? The first thing to do is to acknowledge the presence and activity of God in us, in the problem, and in all the people connected with the problem.

There is always some present action to take. It might seem small, insignificant, but we must take it. The solution to a problem always involves a series of small, seemingly insignificant steps. If, however, there is absolutely nothing we can do in the outer, then our guidance is to do nothing. "But," you may say, "if there is nothing I can do at present about my problem, how do I keep from thinking about it and letting it get me down?" You and only you are the one who can decide what you will think about. The way to stop thinking about apples is to think about horses. The way to stop thinking about your problem is to decide to think about something else. Expand your vision, get active with something else, in a new direction. Follow the advice that Emmet Fox gives in that helpful pamphlet *The Golden Key*, "When you are inclined to think about your problem, think about God instead."

How do you think about God? *What* do you think about God? *Know* that God is a very real presence, sometimes an invisible activity, ever working toward the perfect solution to your problem. Compose an affirmation such as the following to repeat everytime you find yourself stewing and worrying and tempted to dwell in the past: *I put the past behind me. I face forward with my hand in God's, knowing that I am unerringly guided into right action and a successful outcome. I am grateful.*

From this point in consciousness you are ready to release all the negative elements in your mental rear-vision mirror. You are ready to proceed even further into the positive energy, the unlimited possibilities, the joyful victory of the *now* moment.

PHASE 2 - LIFT YOUR VISION!

Everything begins in the mind. Nothing just pops into being overnight. It begins with an idea and grows as the idea accumulates thought sub-stance so that we can mentally envision and feel it. How do we find the right idea to plant and nur-ture in our portion of the fertile soil of universal Mind? It's easy. It just takes a little time of quiet and introspection.

We begin by finding a quiet place where we can be alone for an hour or so. In this fast-paced, responsibility-ridden life, this may not be as easy as it sounds. But we can arrange it if that inner sense of dissatisfaction, that urging to come up higher, is strong enough in our consciousness. We take time to sort through the various imag-inary circumstances that we can call up into our field of consciousness—those that would make us feel happy, contented, satisfied, fulfilled. We can practice mentally seeing and emotionally feeling ourself experiencing this good, actively enjoying and expressing in this situation.

Mentally seeing, giving our attention to a chosen goal will subtly, automatically change our way of thinking. Because thought is a formative power, we will find ourself acting in a different way and attracting people, events, and circum-stances into our life that draw us toward our higher good, our goal, our expanded vision of life-to-be.

Imagination—the scissors of the mind—is like ordinary scissors, in that it cuts out things, cuts off unwanted ends. It shapes stars or hearts or

144

figures, according to how we use the "scissors."
Our tremendous power of imagination does the
very same thing with the everywhere-present substance of God. Do we want a "broken heart"?
Then we can just imagine people letting us down,
be suspicious of anyone who tries to get close,
and expect to be turned off. If we look down
broken-heart lane, we will find ourself there. On
the other hand, we can carve out a heart overflow-
ing with love and happiness. We can carve out a
cornucopia, a horn of plenty, with the scissors of
our imagination.

Jesus did some mighty deeds 2,000 years ago.
So mighty were His actions that religion calls
them miracles, but Jesus didn't. He merely did
what the occasion called for, did what needed
doing. Not only did He *not* think of these acts as
miracles, but He flatly assured His listeners, "He
who believes in me will also do the works that I
do; and greater works than these will he do"—
John 14:12.

When do you think He meant you to do these
things and "even greater works"? Do you think
that He meant you should wait until you get to
heaven up in the sky? Do you think He meant
some future incarnation when the outer facts of
your life are more conducive to your success? Do
you think He meant you must join a certain religious group and submit to a certain ritual?

Jesus was talking about the here and now—the

145

powers and potential that lie within us here and *now* as a child of our Father-God. He meant us to "have life, and have it abundantly"—*in the now moment.*

Whatever it is that will make us feel fulfilled, free from fear, satisfied, as a child of God should be, we must reach for it in our consciousness. We must put the past firmly behind us, where it belongs, and redirect our spiritual energies to the glorious future—a future that has its beginnings in the beautiful now. Whatever we look upon will draw us toward it!

I lift my gaze above the horizon of my present circumstances to my unlimited potential as a child of God, a center of all-accomplishing spiritual energy and intelligence.

Get Into Heaven

The terms "kingdom of heaven" and "kingdom of God" can be used interchangeably. Each means the "place" where God is. The chief reason for the two terms given in the New Testament is that Matthew always refers to the kingdom of heaven, whereas Mark and Luke refer to it as the kingdom of God.

In Truth, we know that the kingdom of God is not a specific geographical place. That is, it is not a separate physical realm existing somewhere in the sky or in the far reaches of outer space. This was the way of old-time religion, though many persons still believe it. We need a fresh perspective of the kingdom, based on the eternal Truth of Jesus' teachings.

The kingdom idea was and is a very important part of the teachings of Jesus. In the Four Gospels, there are 113 references to the kingdom of heaven and the kingdom of God. Not one of Jesus' descriptions of the kingdom places this

147

kingdom in the sky. Not once does He mention angels, harps, or streets of gold.

> The kingdom of heaven is like treasure hidden in a field, which a man found and covered up; then in his joy he goes and sells all that he has and buys that field—Matthew 13:44.

> Again, the kingdom of heaven is like a merchant in search of fine pearls, who, on finding one pearl of great value, went and sold all that he had and bought it—Matthew 13:45.

> It [the kingdom of God] is like a grain of mustard seed, which, when sown upon the ground, is the smallest of all the seeds on earth; yet when it is sown it grows up and becomes the greatest of all shrubs, and puts forth large branches, so that the birds of the air can make nests in its shade—Mark 4:31.

Do these descriptions sound like a land of golden streets in the far reaches of outer space? Certainly it is difficult to interpret these passages as referring to a place in the sky with angels and trumpets. In Luke Jesus speaks so plainly, so specifically that it is a wonder how intelligent people can read it and still claim that the kingdom of heaven is an after-death place, somewhere removed from this planet, this life.

> *Being asked by the Pharisees when the king-*
> *dom of God was coming, he answered them,*
> *"The kingdom of God is not coming with*
> *signs to be observed; nor will they say, 'Lo,*
> *here it is!' or 'There!' for behold, the kingdom*
> *of God is in the midst of you"—Luke 17:20,*
> *21.*

Still, we can understand how the kingdom of
God came to be placed in the sky, in the sweet by-
and-by. It gave people hope. Life was hard, filled
with wars, famine, plagues, poverty. What a selling point for missionaries and evangelists, to be
able to promise an after-death life of prosperity,
wholeness, peace, freedom from all hardship and
trouble—even a crown for each head, if the
listeners would only join the church and obey its
rules and rituals.

If getting into heaven were that simple, why
didn't Jesus state it that way, instead of likening
the kingdom to finding pearls or sowing a mustard
seed? It seems plain enough that the kingdom of
God is within us. That understanding of Jesus'
teaching tells us *where* to find the kingdom.

But now, *what* is the kingdom of God? If the
kingdom of God is within us, then we can say that
it is not a physical place, it is nonphysical. Physical means something tangible that we can see,

touch, taste, smell, or hear. We have five senses to feed us information from the physical world. Nonphysical means something that we cannot see, hear, touch, taste, or smell. Nonphysical elements are, for example, thoughts, emotions, ideas, mental attitudes, beliefs—things that have to do with the mind. It is in this area that we search for the kingdom of God. The kingdom of God is a consciousness we enter into when our thoughts, attitudes, emotions, ideas, and beliefs are in tune with God-Mind.

How do we get into the kingdom of God? This is perhaps the most important question of the three. We can talk about the kingdom of God within people, within ourself until we are blue in the face. We can admire the logic of it and even smugly quote Luke 17:21: "Behold, the kingdom of God is in the midst of you." But unless we do something about getting our mind in tune with it, we are very much like the character in one of Aesop's Fables, "The Miser and His Gold":

> *Once upon a time there was a Miser who used to hide his gold at the foot of a tree in his garden; but every week he used to go and dig it up and gloat over his gains. A robber, who had noticed this, went and dug up the gold and decamped with it. When the Miser next came to gloat over his treasures, he found nothing but the empty hole. He tore his*

hair, and raised such an outcry that all the neighbours came around him, and he told them how he used to come and visit his gold. "Did you ever take any of it out?" asked one of them.

"Nay," said he, "I only came to look at it."

"Then come again and look at the hole," said a neighbour; "it will do you just as much good."

WEALTH UNUSED MIGHT AS WELL NOT EXIST.

The kingdom of God is within us, but if we only talk and think about it, never using its power and wisdom for good, its wealth might as well not exist. We can enter, enjoy, and express the kingdom of God with all its power and wisdom through a subjective experience called meditation.

The kingdom of God is within, but not in the stomach, liver, or any specific physical part. It is in our mind, our consciousness. Spending time in our mind is meditative prayer. There is no "right" way to meditate. We do well if, in the beginning, we just sit quietly and get acquainted with our mind and its contents—thoughts, feelings, images, and memories.

To most of us, mind is a great unknown territory; it is strange to us because we spend so little time in it. We would rather do almost anything than simply be alone and think. We gladly read a book, telephone someone, take a ride, go to a movie, eat, sleep, and even do strenuous work. But to have to walk in the shadowy and unfamiliar territory of the mind is something many of us do not want to do.

The way to overcome this avoidance is to simply begin. The only thing we need to practice when we sit quietly and turn our attention away from the outer and toward the inner depths of the mind is to *observe our thoughts;* not to let them carry us away, not to identify with them, not to relive a memory that comes up but to simply observe.

This may be difficult at first. We may find that we identify with a certain train of thought and away we go with it. Soon we are not really "here" in the now at all, but off with the flow of those thoughts. Five minutes later, we "get off the train" and know inwardly that we did it again—we let a thought or memory capture our interest and carry us away rather than standing back and observing what we were thinking, imaging, and feeling.

After a time we begin to feel "at home" in the mind and then the kingdom of God begins to seep into our thoughts, attitudes, and feelings. A difficult to describe phenomenon called "understanding" occurs. Understanding, the Bible assures us, is more valuable than silver or gold. And yet, it cannot be bought or sold. Understanding "bubbles up" from within. Spiritual understanding provides the answer to every experience that confronts us. It opens the door to strength, guidance, and healing when they are needed. Problems become opportunities to work with God, and working with God is the process through which every problem is correctly solved, the process that yields results of greater good, fuller mastery, and expanded understanding.

How do we get into heaven? Not by dying, not by joining a church, not by being sprinkled instead of dunked, or dunked instead of sprinkled. We get into heaven by seeking—moment by moment, day by day, challenge by challenge—to get our mind and inner reactions in *tune,* with Truth. Then we find that heaven is not in the sweet by-and-by, but right here in the eternal *now.*

As we enter this *now* in consciousness, we grow more accustomed to the kingdom of heaven, this spiritual atmosphere within us. We begin to have a deeper awareness of the nature of God as Spirit, as Life, and as Infinite Mind. To explore a litte more in this inner kingdom, let's work with the thought that the life we are aware of as *our* life is the same life that is expressing through all other persons and all forms of life. The mind that we are aware of as our mind is one with the same Mind that is expressing through all the universe. *All life is one.* We are but a focalized point of expression of that one universal Life. All mind is one and we are a point of light in the universal Mind.

We realize that in that one universal Mind is the *kingdom*—the potential in us for all wholeness, all wisdom. In God-Mind we live and move and have our being; the answer to every problem lies in this realm. When we turn within to affirm or realize our oneness with Infinite Wisdom, that wisdom flows to and through us, subtly and intuitively guiding us into right and appropriate action. It is so simple, so easy. And yet, perhaps that is just why we don't go to God first with what we think are difficult life problems. Prayer seems too simple, too easy, too childish. And perhaps, too, this is why Jesus, knowing the human reaction, said, "Unless you turn and become like children, you will never enter the kingdom of heaven"—Matthew 18:2.

Admittedly, living a spiritually oriented life requires adaptation. We have to become acquainted with our faculty of intuition. We are so outer-oriented that we feel all teaching or guidance must come from without—from what we read or from what someone tells us. The word *intuition*, however, means "the power or faculty of attaining to direct knowledge or cognition without evident rational thought and inference."

We must accept the idea that teaching or instruction can come from within us. Learning to trust divine insight from within involves learning to trust ourself. God's guidance comes from within us, through our own thoughts and feelings.

Let's examine the Bible verses that reveal the pearl of great price that is found right within us, the discovery of which will cause us to abandon all the other means we have depended upon for our security, prosperity, and well-being. First we turn to Mark for a description of the beginning of Jesus' three-year ministry:

> *Jesus came into Galilee, preaching the gospel of God, and saying, "The time is fulfilled, and the kingdom of God is at hand; repent, and believe in the gospel"—Mark 1:14, 15.*

The word *gospel* means *good news.* So, *Jesus came preaching the good news of the kingdom of God!* Good news is what we all want. And the kingdom of God certainly is good news!

Then there is another action to be considered—repentance. To repent means to change our mind, our thinking, our beliefs, and our behavior. Our actions spring out of and are the result of what we think and believe. The Phillips translation of this verse omits the word *repent* and reads: "You must change your hearts and minds and believe the Good News."

For centuries the people to whom Jesus was speaking had been waiting for the kingdom of

God to be established on earth by some mighty warrior-messiah, such as King David. Yet Jesus arose from their midst not with armies, but with life-giving teachings, saying in effect, Get ready, the kingdom of God is at hand—very near—so quickly abandon your old belief.

In the 17th chapter of Luke, Jesus had been teaching for quite some time, and the people were ready for the real "blockbuster" of limited beliefs. The secret was let out. The long waiting was ended. There it was, out in the open at last, the Truth about the kingdom of God was revealed. The misunderstanding about some sort of worldly government to be ruled by a religious warrior king was finally corrected. Jesus said the kingdom of God is in the midst of us.

For some, the term "kingdom of God" excites little or nor response. It has become just another part of religious jargon that one gets so used to hearing. Therefore, let's use terms that may have new impact on us, such as, cosmic consciousness, or a place of infinite wisdom and power, or simply God indwelling. The kingdom of God is God's dwelling place, and if the kingdom of God is in us, then God certainly dwells in us.

Jesus used the word *kingdom* because it was a familiar and meaningful concept to the Jews He was teaching. Their history was filled with references to one kingdom or another. They knew that a kingdom was a place. Jesus revealed the nature of that place within. The only qualification Jesus mentions for getting into this "place" within is that we *repent*. What associations does the word *repent* call forth in us? The sawdust trail? Drunkards throwing away their bottles? People confessing to immoral thoughts or actions? Repent means to change our mind—to change it at a very deep level, the level of *what we believe to be true*—and to act accordingly. If we believe that outer conditions have power over our life and well-being—power to prosper and power to destroy—that belief must be changed. This is repentance! The teaching of Jesus is that we need to repent and believe the good news.

Such repentance changes our outer behavior. When we repent of the belief that outer conditions have power over us, we no longer run scared. After repentance we no longer try to manipulate people by pretending that we are helping them when we are really only interested in helping ourself. When we are sincere we don't have to play many different roles in order to set up favorable outer conditions. We can be patient, serene, and at peace with ourself and the world. The outer negative habits can be changed into positive responses to life because the mind has been changed by repentance. Repentance changes our behavior because it changes the direction of our dependency from outward to inward.

What we place our faith in, we *depend*

upon—and that dependency directs our life. Repentance means abandoning faith in and dependence on ever-changing outer appearances; it means learning to depend on the kingdom of God within us. It means that we activate our spiritual potential in the fullest, most effective, most wonderful way. It means that through our uplifted consciousness, we can joyously live in the kingdom of heaven in this life.

Printed U.S.A.

141-F-4769-75C-2-81